# EDWARDIAN ERA
## Miniatures in 1:12 Scale

·EX·LIBRIS·

_____

_____

# Edwardian Era Miniatures

## in 1:12 Scale

**Ann Sutcliffe** reviews Jane Harrop's delightful book 'Edwardian Era Miniatures in 1:12 Scale'.

Jane Harrop has been making miniatures for the past 17 years, selling them at fairs and through her website. Jane also writes articles and runs workshops both in person and on-line. In this book, Jane covers the Edwardian era from the death of Queen Victoria through to the end of the First World War.

### Projects featured

The projects in this book take you through a typical middle class home of the time, with over 40 step-by-step projects. These are exclusively 1/12th scale; although many are fairly easily halved to 1/24th scale. You enter Jane's Edwardian dolls house through the hallway, and move on room by room making the furniture and accessories as you go. As you progress through the rooms in the book, a detailed description of the era, the wallpapers, floor coverings, curtains and fabrics are all explained. Each project within the room setting is laid out with a brief history, the dimensions, and a list of materials required. This is followed by step-by-step instructions, diagrams and photographs. A project

for a large item like a table will be followed by a smaller project to make the vase of roses to sit on top, thus providing an interesting and diverse array of projects.

### Methods and techniques

Whilst working through each room in the house, Jane teaches different methods and how to use various materials to achieve the look. Predominantly, the pieces are made from wood but there is also metal and clay work, plus the use of paper, plastics, card, beads, paint and fabric. The book is a veritable masterclass, with many techniques for a modern day miniaturist to acquire in order to fill their dolls house with their own individually crafted items.

The 180 page book is in paperback format. The printing is clear and legible with easy to follow instructions, clear photos and accurate templates. The pages are dotted with extra photos, ideas, and further 'why not try' suggestions to alter and embellish your work. At the back of the book are all the scale templates along with descriptions and photos of materials and

equipment, techniques and most importantly, suppliers. All in all, it is a thoroughly good read and a first-rate workbook to add to your miniature DIY library.

### Tried and tested project

As I like to check out the instructions in all DIY books before giving the thumbs up, I have made one of the projects in the book. As all dolls houses need beds, I chose to make Jane's cast iron single Edwardian bed. It is constructed from a mixture of materials including wood, plastic tubing, wire, and Hama beads, and of course it needs bedding, but I have to say I am extremely pleased with the result!

**INFORMATION**
A copy of the book is available from Jane Harrop.
T: 01625 873117
E: janeharrop@tesco.net
W: janeharrop.co.uk

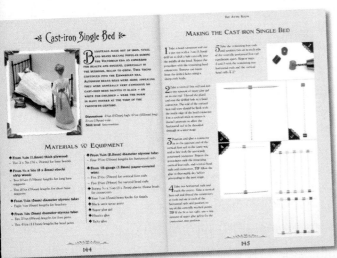

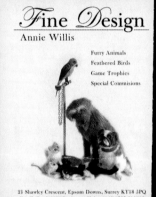
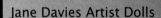

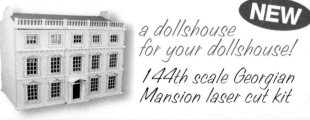

# Edwardian Era
## Miniatures in 1:12 Scale

## Jane Harrop

GUILD OF MASTER
CRAFTSMAN PUBLICATIONS

*For my girls, Amy and Lucy*
*With love*

First published 2011 by
**GUILD OF MASTER CRAFTSMAN PUBLICATIONS LTD**
Castle Place, 166 High Street, Lewes,
East Sussex BN7 1XU

Text © Jane Harrop, 2011
Copyright in the Work © GMC Publications Ltd, 2011

ISBN 978-1-86108-806-2

Whilst every effort has been made to obtain permission from the
copyright holders for all material used in this book, the publishers will
be pleased to hear from anyone who has not been appropriately
acknowledged and to make the correction in future reprints.

The publishers and author can accept no legal responsibility for any
consequences arising from the application of information, advice or
instructions given in this publication.

A catalogue record for this book is available from the British Library.

Publisher JONATHAN BAILEY
Production Manager JIM BULLEY
Managing Editor GERRIE PURCELL
Project Editors GILL PARRIS, JUDITH CHAMBERLAIN-WEBBER
Managing Art Editor GILDA PACITTI
Photographer ANDREW PERRIS

Colour origination by GMC REPROGRAPHICS
Printed and bound by HUNG HING OFFSET LTD

# Contents

Introduction **8**

### THE HALLWAY

Arts & Crafts Hallstand **14**

Plant Stand **18**

Potted Fern Plant **20**

Decorative Metalware **22**

Craftsman Hall Bench **25**

Arts & Crafts Occasional Table **28**

### THE DINING ROOM

Craftsman Dining Table **34**

Craftsman Dining Chair **36**

Craftsman Serving Table **38**

Bowls & Stands **40**

Reception Room Fireplace **42**

Over-mantel Mirror **46**

Vase of Roses **48**

### THE LIVING ROOM

Arts & Crafts Corner Sofa **54**

Arts & Crafts Reclining Armchair **58**

Arts & Crafts Lady's Writing Desk **61**

Arts & Crafts Desk Chair **64**

Desk Accessories **66**

Gramophone **70**

Arts & Crafts Gramophone Table **74**

Wall Shelves **76**

Tiffany Table Lamp **78**

Brownie Box Camera **80**

## THE KITCHEN

## THE BEDROOM

## THE ATTIC ROOM

Kitchen Table 86

Sink & Draining Board 89

Plate Rack 92

Kitchen Dresser 94

Kitchen Fireplace Surround 98

Kitchen Range 100

Kitchenware 105

Dressing Table 112

Dressing Table Accessories 117

Double Bed 120

Bedroom Fireplace 123

Wardrobe 127

Chest of Drawers 136

Tabletop Mirror 139

Washstand 142

Cast-iron Single Bed 144

Pull Horse 148

Craftsman Child's Rocking Chair 150

Templates 153

Equipment & Materials 169

Basic Techniques 177

Suppliers 180

Bibliography/ About the Author/ Acknowledgements 182

Index 183

# Introduction

THE EDWARDIAN ERA BEGAN in Britain when Edward VII inherited the throne from Queen Victoria in 1901 and, although he died in 1910, it is generally accepted to have lasted until the end of World War I in 1918. In America, the beginning of the twentieth century was known as the progressive era and was named after dedicated progressives (reformists) who were committed to improving and reforming American life.

It was a time of rapid social and political changes and there was a huge gap between the rich and the poor. In Europe the period was known as the Belle Époque (beautiful era) and for the very rich and privileged it was a time of overindulgent extravagance epitomised in Britain by King Edward VII.

On both sides of the Atlantic, reform movements campaigned to improve the working and living conditions of low-paid workers and the impoverished. Around the world women crusaded for women's suffrage – the legal right for all women to vote.

The era was a period of scientific and technological progress with the invention of electricity and the discovery of radioactivity. Travel was revolutionised with the first ground-breaking flight, the mass production of motor cars by the Ford Motor Company and street running electric tramways.

Influenced by America, communities developed in the suburbs in Britain and combined the best of town and country living. Modern houses were built in open leafy spaces and attracted the health-conscious Edwardians. In Britain and America newly built homes were smaller than their Victorian counterparts to suit the growing trend of raising smaller families and having live-out servants. Almost ninety percent of homes were rented and it became respectable for the expanding middle classes to live in the suburbs and commute into work. Leisure time was important to the Edwardians and healthy outdoor activities predominated. Advances in transport encouraged day trips to the seaside and country.

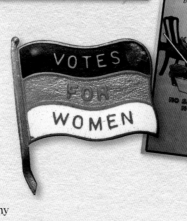

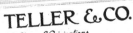

# IMPORTANT INFORMATION ABOUT MEASUREMENTS

The standard dolls' house scale is 1:12, originally based on imperial measurements: in 1:12 scale, one inch represents one foot. Although many craftspeople now use metric measurements, dolls' house hobbyists in Britain and especially America still use feet and inches. For each project, imperial measurements are given first, followed by their metric equivalent in brackets. Accuracy to the millimetre is generally inappropriate, and metric measurements have been rounded up or down for convenience. Never mix imperial and metric measurements – always use one or the other.

NOTE: In some of the projects in this book metric conversions may vary slightly to ensure a good fit.

There were two main influences on the interior decoration and furnishings in the home. The Arts & Crafts reform movement promoted hand-made craftsmanship, which had been lost to the excess mass production of the Victorian age, and Art Nouveau style introduced the concept of using simple, elongated rectilinear and curvilinear forms.

Publications encouraged the Edwardians to spend their earnings on stylish home furnishing as a reflection of their status. In this book you will be shown how to make turn-of-the-century one-twelfth scale furniture and accessories through step-by-step instructions and photographs. The projects have been arranged room by room and we begin in the hallway.

Craftsman Hall Bench - page 25

Decorative
Metalware
- page 22

# THE HALLWAY

# IN THE HALLWAY

ONE OF THE MOST SIGNIFICANT changes made to newly built homes during the Edwardian era was larger hallways. Previously, in many Victorian houses, hallways were just constricted passageways. It was the Arts & Crafts movement who prompted the reform for hallways to become more spacious, their inspiration being taken from Gothic architecture and the great halls of that time which were used as a living space.

Larger building plots in the suburbs and garden cities enabled many newly built homes a wider frontage than before, allowing space for a bigger hallway. It became fashionable for the hallway to be used as a living space which became known as a sitting hall. Fireplaces were often fitted to ensure the home was warm and welcoming to visitors. Publications offered tips and advice on hall decoration and advised that furnishings be kept simple.

The Edwardian hallway would have been fashionably decorated to impress visitors and reflect its owner's status and wealth. One of the most distinguishing features of the hall was the solid tiled decorative floor laid in geometric patterns and edged with border tiles. Not only were they visually attractive and in vogue, they were also reasonably cheap, and easy to clean. As hygiene was such a major concern to the Edwardians, this was a particularly important factor.

The hallway was the only room in which the Victorian trend for rooms to be decorated in strong, dark colours remained and internal woodwork was often kept dark. The dado rail, previously a feature in all rooms, also survived only in the hallway. Durable wallpapers covered the wall below the dado rail and varnished embossed papers like lincrusta and anaglypta were very common. Between the dado rail and the picture rail patterned wallpapers with naturalistic themes, particularly floral, in Arts & Crafts and Art Nouveau designs were extremely popular. The area above the picture rail was often painted white or cream so that it merged in with the ceiling colour.

Although electrical supplies were available during the Edwardian era many homes still used gas lighting. Fittings were usually the same for both and pendant lamps and glass bowls suspended on chains were often found in the hallway.

Other distinctive features were decorative, stained glass windows and door panels with Art Nouveau stylised floral patterns and simply designed square newel posts and balusters on staircases. These features all followed traditional Arts & Crafts designs.

# ❧ Arts & Crafts Hallstand ❧

**A**RTS & CRAFTS FURNITURE WAS GENERALLY MADE OUT OF NATIVE WOODS SUCH AS OAK AND THEN WAXED. ITS STYLE WAS FUNCTIONAL, BASED ON SIMPLE DESIGNS AND CONSTRUCTED USING TRADITIONAL JOINERY TECHNIQUES. PIERCED HEART MOTIFS WERE OFTEN USED AS DECORATION. THE HALLSTAND WAS AN ESSENTIAL PIECE OF FURNITURE IN THE MIDDLE-CLASS EDWARDIAN HALLWAY FOR ACCOMMODATING OUTDOOR GARMENTS AND ACCESSORIES.

**Dimensions** 6⁹⁄₁₆in (167mm) high; 3⅜in (86mm) wide; 1¹⁄₁₆in (27mm) deep
**Skill level** Advanced
**Templates** Page 153

# MATERIALS & EQUIPMENT

♠ **From ³⁄₃₂in (2.5mm) thick obechi sheet wood:**
- 2¾ x ¾in (70 x 19mm) for tray base
- 2½ x 1¹⁄₁₆in (64 x 27mm) for back

♠ **From ¹⁄₁₆in (1.5mm) thick obechi sheet wood:**
- 3¼ x ³⁄₁₆in (83 x 5mm) for capping
- Two ¾ x ³⁄₁₆in (19 x 5mm) for tray side trim
- 2⅝ x ³⁄₁₆in (67 x 5mm) for tray front trim
- Two ¾ x ½in (19 x 13mm) for box sides
- ⅞ x ¾in (22 x 19mm) for box base
- 1⅛ x ¹⁵⁄₁₆in (29 x 24mm) for box lid
- Two ⁵⁄₁₆ x ¼in (8 x 6mm) for leg caps

♠ **From ¹⁄₃₂in (1mm) thick obechi sheet wood:**
- 2½ x 1⅜in (64 x 35mm) for mirror back
- 2½ x ⁹⁄₁₆in (64 x 14mm) for back panel
- ⅞ x ¾in (22 x 19mm) for lid clip

♠ **From ½ x ⅛in (13 x 3mm) obechi strip wood:**
- 2⅝in (67mm) length for front
- 3¼in (83mm) length for top

♠ **From ⁵⁄₁₆ x ⅛in (8 x 3mm) obechi strip wood:**
- Two 1³⁄₁₆in (30mm) lengths for decorative rails
- 2½in (64mm) length for tray back

♠ **From ¼ x ⅛in (6 x 3mm) obechi strip wood:**

– Two 6in (152mm) length for back legs

– 3¼in (82mm) length for upper cross rail

– 2½in (64mm) length for lower cross rail

– 1⅜in (35mm) length for upright rail

– Two ¾in (19mm) lengths for side rails

♠ **From ³⁄₁₆ x ⅛in (5 x 3mm) obechi strip wood:**

– Two 2⅜in (60mm) lengths for front legs

♠ ½in (13mm) diameter wood dowel

♠ **From ³⁄₆₄in (1mm) thick plastic sheet mirror:**

– 2½ x 1⅜in (64 x 35mm) for mirror

♠ Five ½ x ½in (13 x 13mm) wall tiles

♠ Four ⁹⁄₁₆in (14mm) wooden belaying pins for pegs

♠ Two ⁹⁄₁₆in (14mm) diameter aluminium dinner plates for drip trays

♠ Oak wood stain

♠ Beeswax polish

♠ Tacky glue

# MAKING THE ARTS & CRAFTS HALLSTAND

**1** Transfer the hallstand's back leg (**A**) template to the two back legs. Make a groove in each back leg ¼in (6mm) wide and ¹⁄₁₆in (1.5mm) deep, by first scoring along the marked lines and then using a needle file to make a channel in between the scored lines.

**2** Turn the back legs over and transfer the drill hole position from the hallstand's back leg (**B**) template. Use a pin vice with a ¹⁄₁₆in (1.5mm) drill bit to drill part way through the wood pieces.

**3** Take the upper cross rail and transfer the template. Repeat the procedures at step 1 to make grooves. **OPTIONAL** Carefully mitre the ends of the wood piece (see page 178).

**4** Take the front wood piece, transfer the template and cut out. Wind and glue a piece of fine-grade sandpaper around the dowel to make a sanding tool.

**5** Measure ³⁄₁₆in (5mm) down from the top on each angled edge. Position the sanding tool on the pencil marks and sand approximately ⅛in (3mm) down into the wood as shown. Use fine-grade sandpaper to round the top edges on each side of the indentations to produce a smooth, continuous edge. ☞

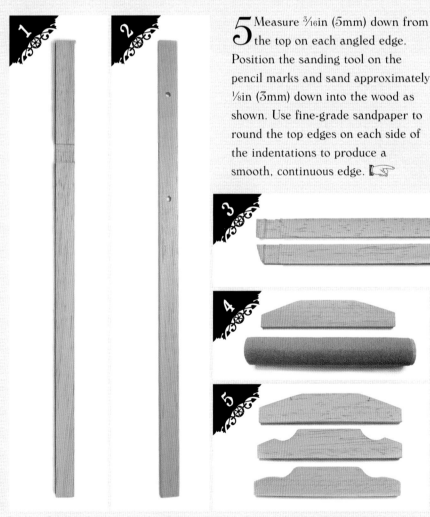

6 Take the top wood piece and measure and mark ¾in (19mm) inwards from each end. Repeat the procedures at step 5 to make indentations. Slightly trim the wood widthways at each end to create a stepped border.

7 Take the tray base wood piece and transfer the template on to it. Use a pin vice with a ³⁄₆₄in (1mm) drill bit to drill a series of holes on the inside of each marked circle. Use a sharp craft knife to remove the waste from the circles. Sand the openings smooth using a needle file and fine-grade sandpaper.

8 Take the decorative rails and draw a small heart shape in the same position on each. Repeat step 7 using a ¹⁄₃₂in (1mm) drill bit. Sand and apply wood stain to all of the wooden components.

9 Position and glue the upper cross rail into the notches on the back of the legs. Fix the mirror back wood piece on to the back of the mirror and then position and glue into the gap at the top of the construction. Take the two pierced decorative rails and position and glue equidistant apart below the upper cross rail. Glue the lower cross rail immediately below.

10 Position and glue the back panel on top of the back piece with the bottom edges flush: the gap of ½in (13mm) above is for tiles at a later stage. Glue this immediately below the back lower cross rail. Position the upright rail centrally below, followed by the tray back wood piece, and glue into place.

11 Trim the capping wood strip to fit the straight edges on the top wood piece, with a small overlap at each end. Fix the capping into place, so the back of the strips are flush with the back of the top piece. Glue at the top of the construction, with an equal overlap at each end.

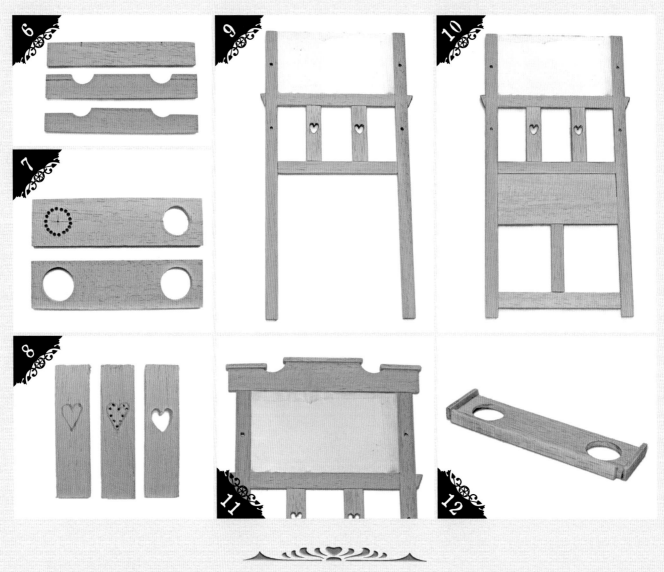

12 Take the tray base wood piece and position and glue the tray side trims on to the short outside edges of the tray base piece. Position and glue the tray front trim centrally on to one long edge on the tray base wood piece. All bottom edges are flush. Polish all of the constructions and all remaining wood pieces with beeswax polish. **TIP** Avoid polishing the ends of the loose strip wood pieces.

13 Position and glue the tray construction on top of the tray back wood piece, so all bottom edges run in line. Stand the ends of the side rails on to the back legs, the bottom edges in line with the bottom edge of the back and back panel wood pieces. Position the side rails $\frac{1}{16}$in (1.5mm) from the outside edge of the back legs and glue into place.

14 Position and glue the tiles into the sunken section on the back of the hallstand. Place the box side pieces on to the short edges of the box base wood piece. Position and glue centrally on to the back panel. The bottom of the box should be flush with the bottom edge of the back panel. Position and glue the lid clip on top of the box lid, one long edge on each should be flush and all other edges should overlap equally.

15 Position and glue the front legs, wide side down, to rest on the ends of the side rails and against the front of the tray base. The front legs should protrude from the bottom edge of the tray by $\frac{3}{16}$in (5mm). Position and glue the front wood piece between the front legs, so the top edge is flush with the top of the un-lidded box. Position and glue the leg caps on top of each front leg with the grain of the wood pieces running horizontally and allowing an equal overlap on each side.

16 To make the hooks, remove part of the straight section of the wood from the belaying pins leaving $\frac{1}{16}$in (1.5mm) attached to the turned head and glue the straight ends into the holes in the back legs. Glue the drip trays to rest in the cut-out sections in the tray base and remove the protective covering on the mirror. Rest the lid on top of the box, with the lid clip facing downwards and the flush edge against the back of the hallstand.

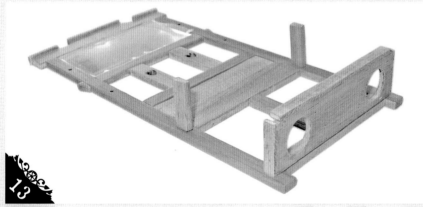

# Plant Stand

ALTHOUGH EDWARDIAN HOMES WERE USUALLY LESS CLUTTERED THAN HOMES FROM THE VICTORIAN ERA, SMALL PIECES OF DECORATIVE FURNITURE WERE STILL POPULAR AND AFFORDABLE. MANY NEWSPAPERS AND MAGAZINES PUBLISHED ARTICLES THAT SUGGESTED FURNITURE SHOULD BE SIMPLE, LIGHT AND DELICATE WITH MINIMAL ORNAMENTATION. A PLANT STAND HOLDING A POTTED FERN WAS CONSIDERED A SUITABLE PIECE OF FURNITURE FOR AN EDWARDIAN HALLWAY OR LIVING ROOM.

**Dimensions** 3$\frac{7}{32}$in (82mm) high; $\frac{7}{8}$in (22mm) wide; $\frac{7}{8}$in (22mm) deep
**Skill level** Beginner
**Template** Page 153

# MATERIALS & EQUIPMENT

♠ **From ⅛in (3mm) thick mahogany sheet wood:**

– Four ½ x ½in (13 x 13mm) lengths for top supports

♠ **From ³⁄₃₂in (2.5mm) thick mahogany sheet wood:**

– ⅞ x ⅞in (22 x 22mm) for top

♠ **From ¹⁄₁₆in (1.5mm) thick mahogany sheet wood:**

– ¾ x ¾in (19 x 19mm) for shelf

♠ **From ⅛ x ⅛in (3 x 3mm) mahogany strip wood:**

– Four 3⅛in (79mm) lengths for legs

– Four ½in (13mm) lengths for shelf supports

♠ Beeswax polish

♠ Tacky glue

# MAKING THE PLANT STAND

1 Transfer the shelf template on to the shelf wood piece and cut out. To prevent the wood splitting, first cut against the grain, using either mitre cutters or a craft knife, and then cut with the grain of the wood. Lightly sand the surfaces on all sides of the mahogany pieces to produce a smooth finish. Do not alter the shape and sizes of the wood pieces.

2 Position and glue a top support piece between two legs. The top of the support piece should be flush with the tops of the legs, and the grain of the wood piece should run horizontally between the two

legs. Leave a gap of ½in (13mm) at the bottom of the legs and position and glue a shelf support into place. Repeat the procedure with the remaining two legs, a top support and a shelf support. **TIP** Use a right-angled gluing jig at each stage to ensure the construction dries square.

3 Place a leg construction so it rests on its side. Position and glue a top support and a shelf support against the resting leg in line with the previously positioned pieces. Once dry, glue the lower shelf on top of the shelf supports.

4 Join and glue the two leg constructions together. Once dry, position and glue the remaining support pieces into place. Ensure that all supports continue to run in line with each other.

5 Position and glue the top piece centrally on top of the construction ensuring that the grain of the wood runs in line with the shelf wood piece. Once dry, polish the plant stand with beeswax polish.

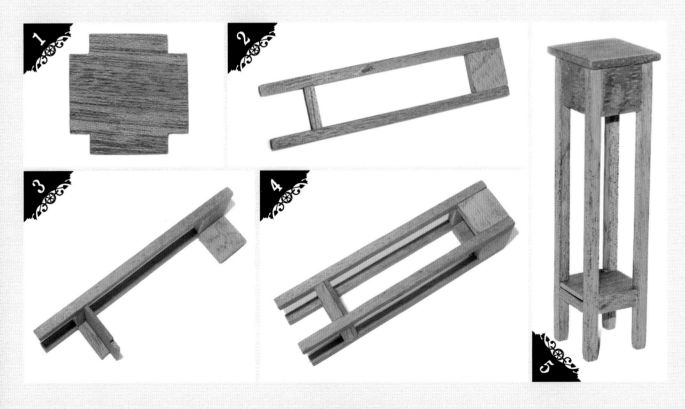

# ⋙ Potted Fern Plant ⋘

**A**T THE TURN OF THE CENTURY, MANY OF THE NEW SUBURBAN AND GARDEN CITY HOMES FOR THE MIDDLE CLASSES WERE BUILT WITH GARDENS ATTACHED. THE EDWARDIANS WERE PASSIONATE ABOUT THE HEALTH BENEFITS OF THE OPEN AIR, AND GARDENING CAME TO BE CONSIDERED AN ACCEPTABLE AND ENJOYABLE PASTIME. SIMPLE, NATURALISTIC AND INEXPENSIVE PLANTS AND FLOWER ARRANGEMENTS WERE THOUGHT TO BRING THE OUTDOORS INTO THE HOME.

**Dimensions**  1⅛in (29mm) high; 2¼in (57mm) wide
**Skill level**  Beginner
**Template**  Page 153

## MATERIALS & EQUIPMENT

- ♠ Leaf green floral tape for leaves
- ♠ 26-gauge (0.45mm) green paper floral wire for stems
- ♠ Dry tea leaves for soil
- ♠ Tacky glue
- ♠ Plant pot (page 22)

## Why not try...

...following the basic method for making the leaves, without forming the fronds, to make an aspidistra plant, popular during the Victorian and Edwardian eras. Make approximately fifteen leaves, and plant leaving some of the stem visible with the largest leaves in the centre and the smallest on the outside.

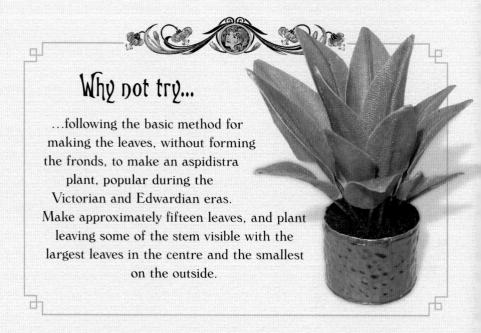

# MAKING THE POTTED FERN PLANT

**1** Cut approximately twenty strips of floral tape into a variety of lengths ranging from 2½in (64mm) to ½in (13mm). Take a piece of the cut tape and fold in half lengthways. Cut a piece of floral wire to measure approximately 1in (25mm) longer than the folded piece of tape.

**2** Re-open the tape and cover one half with a thin and even layer of tacky glue. Lay the wire centrally on top of the adhesive, with the end of the wire approximately ³⁄₆₄in (1mm) short of the fold as shown. Fold the tape over to secure the tape and wire together. Repeat the procedures with the remaining pieces of tape.

**3** Take one of the largest pieces and transfer the leaf template on to the tape and cut out the shape using small sharp scissors. Repeat the procedure with the remaining pieces, altering the span of the leaf as necessary.

**4** Take one of the leaf shapes and holding the wire, cut a series of slits along one side of the leaf up to the central wire and at an angle as shown to form the fronds. Repeat the procedure on the opposite side of the leaf. **TIP** The fronds should be no wider than ³⁄₆₄in (1mm).

**5** Make the fronds realistic by trimming the ends of some to a point or angle. Separate and ruffle the fronds with a cocktail stick. Repeat the procedure with the remaining leaf shapes.

**6** Mix a small amount of dry tea leaves with a little tacky glue and press into the plant pot. Trim the ends of the wires to measure ³⁄₈in (10mm) and immediately start planting the leaves in the plant pot, beginning with the smallest leaves in the centre and finishing with the largest ones on the outside. Once the soil has dried, bend and re-ruffle the leaves into realistic shapes.

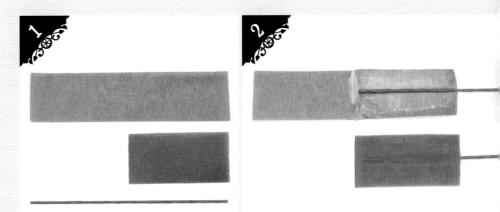

# ❧ Decorative Metalware ❧

THE ARTS & CRAFTS MOVEMENT WAS RESPONSIBLE FOR THE REVIVAL OF HAND-PRODUCED DECORATIVE METALWARE AFTER ITS DECLINE DUE TO INDUSTRIALIZATION. CRAFTSMEN MADE PIECES FROM PRECIOUS METALS SUCH AS SILVER AND BRONZE, AS WELL AS FROM PEWTER, COPPER AND BRASS. METAL WORK WAS EMBOSSED WITH DELICATE CURVED AND FLOWING LINES.

**Dimensions:**
**Plant Pot** 9/16in (14mm) high; 25/32in (20mm) wide
**Box** 1/2in (13mm) high; 1 1/32in (26mm) wide; 21/32in (17mm) deep
**Skill level** Beginner
**Template** Page 153

# MATERIALS & EQUIPMENT

## FOR BOTH ITEMS

♠ Embossing tool

♠ 3/64in (1mm) thick card for pad

♠ Super glue gel

♠ Paper for design pattern

## FOR THE PLANT POT

♠ **From pewter embossing sheet:**

– 2 7/16 x 9/16in (62 x 14mm) for side

– 3/4in (19mm) diameter disc for base

♠ 5/8in (16mm) hard wood dowel or similar cylinder shape for former

♠ Adhesive tape

## FOR THE BOX

♠ **From 1/16in (1.5mm) thick sheet wood:**

– Two 1 x 5/16in (25 x 8mm) for box sides

– Two 1/2 x 5/16in (13 x 8mm) for box ends

– 7/8 x 1/2in (22 x 13mm) for box base

– Two 1 x 3/32in (25 x 2.5mm) for lid sides

– Two 1/2in (13mm) x 3/32in (2.5mm) for lid ends

– 1 x 5/8in (25 x 16mm) for lid

♠ **From 1/32in (1mm) thick sheet wood:**

– Two 1/2 by 9/32in (13 x 7mm) for lid catches

♠ **From pewter embossing sheet:**

– 1 11/32 x 31/32in (34 x 25mm) for lid cover

– 3 5/16 x 5/16in (84 x 8mm) for box cover

♠ Wood stain

♠ Tacky glue

# MAKING THE PLANT POT

1 Place the pewter side piece on top of the card pad and position the edge of a ruler ¹⁄₁₆in (1.5mm) down from one long edge on the pewter strip. Use the biggest end of an embossing tool to draw a line against the edge of the ruler to make an impression in the metal. Repeat the procedure on the same side of the pewter along the opposite edge.

2 Turn the pewter over to reveal two raised lines along the edges of the metal strip. Immediately below the raised lines carefully draw a line using the smallest end of an embossing tool against the edge of a ruler to accentuate the raised edges.

3 Transfer the plant pot design on to a piece of paper. Place the strip of pewter with the raised embossed lines facing downwards on top of the card pad. Trim the paper slightly larger than the design and position and tape the edges of the paper on to the back of the pewter strip, leaving a gap of ¹⁄₈in (3mm) from the end of the pewter to the beginning of the image for the overlap at a later stage.

4 Carefully trace the lines of the pattern using a fine-tipped embossing tool. Remove the paper template to reveal the pattern impressed in the pewter. Re-trace on top of the embossed pattern to gently push out the image further.

**NOTE** The lines above and below the design should not be embossed and are for guidance only.

5 With the raised embossed design facing outwards, carefully wind the pewter around a cylinder shape to form into a ring. Gently open out and secure the un-embossed end of the pewter under the opposite end using a dab of super glue gel. Drop and glue the pewter disc base inside the plant pot.

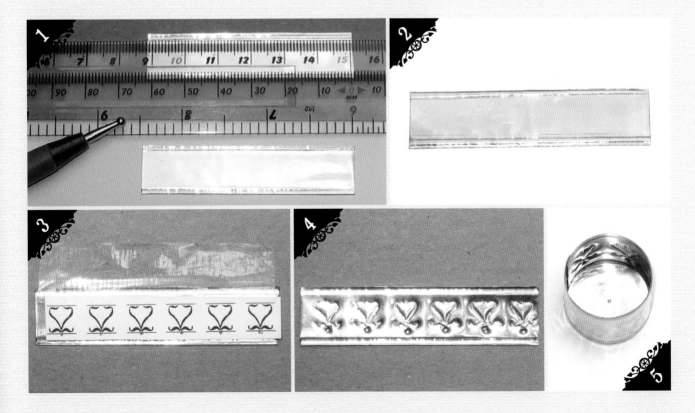

# MAKING THE BOX

**1** Lightly sand and stain the wood pieces. Position and glue the box sides and box end wood pieces on to the outside edge of the box base wood piece. All outside edges are flush. Position and glue the lid catches, wide edge down, inside the box, one at each end. **TIP** Use tacky glue for gluing all the wood pieces securely together.

**2** Position and glue the lid sides and lid ends, narrow edge down, on top of the lid wood piece. All outside edges are flush. Once dry, lightly sand all outside edges of the lid and box to make them smooth and touch up with wood stain.

**3** Transfer the lid cover template on to the lid cover pewter sheet piece and use the smallest end of an embossing tool to score over the dotted lines. Cut out using small sharp scissors. With the indented scored lines facing upwards on the lid cover, follow steps 1–4 for the plant pot to emboss the box design on to the lid cover and box cover pewter pieces as shown.

**4** Fold and glue the box cover pewter strip with the raised embossed design facing outwards around the box, starting and finishing at a corner. Use super glue gel to secure the metal strip.

**5** Position and glue the lid cover pewter piece, with the raised embossed design facing outwards centrally on to the lid top. Carefully fold the pewter on to the sides of the lid and secure using a dab of super glue gel. Trim any excess pewter in the corners using small sharp scissors and then position the lid on top of the box.

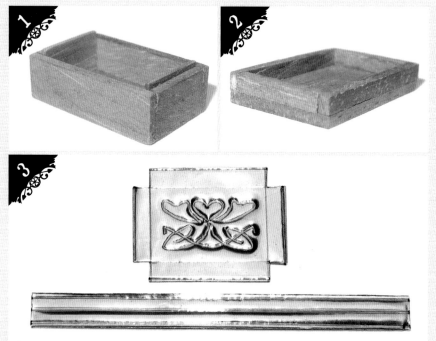

# ❧ Craftsman Hall Bench ☙

AMERICAN FURNITURE DESIGNER GUSTAV STICKLEY PUBLISHED 'THE CRAFTSMAN' MAGAZINE IN AMERICA AT THE BEGINNING OF THE TWENTIETH CENTURY. HE BELIEVED THAT FURNITURE SHOULD BE FUNCTIONAL, SIMPLE AND STURDY, AND REGULARLY INCLUDED HIS DESIGNS IN THE MAGAZINE. STICKLEY TOOK HIS INSPIRATION FROM THE EUROPEAN ARTS & CRAFTS MOVEMENT AND HIS STYLE OF FURNITURE BECAME KNOWN AS 'CRAFTSMAN' AND LATER 'MISSION' STYLE. WITH LARGER HALLWAYS BECOMING POPULAR, SO DID HALL SEATING AND THIS BENCH IS BASED ON ONE OF STICKLEY'S EARLY DESIGNS.

**Dimensions** 3in (76mm) high; 3⁷⁄₁₆in (87mm) wide; 1¹³⁄₁₆in (46mm) deep

**Skill level** Advanced

**Templates** Page 154

# MATERIALS & EQUIPMENT

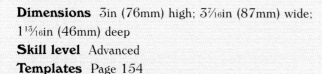

♠ **From ³⁄₁₆in (5mm) thick obechi sheet wood:**
- 3³⁄₁₆ x 1⁹⁄₁₆in (81 x 40mm) for seat

♠ **From ¹⁄₁₆in (1.5mm) thick obechi sheet wood:**
- 3⁷⁄₁₆ x ⁵⁄₈in (87 x 16mm) for back
- 3⁵⁄₁₆ x ⁵⁄₁₆in (84 x 8mm) for cross stretcher
- Four 1¹³⁄₁₆ x ⁵⁄₁₆in (46 x 8mm) for arms and side stretchers

♠ **From ³⁄₁₆ x ³⁄₁₆in (5 x 5mm) obechi strip wood:**
- Two 2¼in (57mm) lengths for front legs
- Two 3in (76mm) lengths for back legs

♠ 4 x 2½in (101 x 64mm) piece of fine glove leather for seat cover

♠ Paper for seat cover template

♠ Low tack double-sided tape

♠ Wood stain

♠ Beeswax polish

♠ Tacky glue

# MAKING THE CRAFTSMAN HALL BENCH

**1** Transfer the seat template on to the seat wood piece and cut out. To prevent the wood splitting, first cut against the grain, using either mitre cutters or a craft knife, and then cut with the grain of the wood.

**2** Transfer the back template, cross stretcher template, arms and side stretcher template on to the corresponding wood pieces and follow the procedures at step 1 to cut out the shoulders and form the tenons.

**3** Transfer the side stretcher template on to the two side stretcher wood pieces. Use a pin vice with a ³⁄₆₄in (1mm) drill bit to drill a series of holes through the wood within the drawn rectangle. Use a sharp craft knife to remove the waste and sand the openings smooth and to size using a needle file.

**4** Transfer the front leg template on to the two front legs. Repeat the procedures at step 3 in order to remove the waste from the mortises (slots).

**5** Transfer the back leg template (**A**) on to the two back legs and repeat the procedures at step 3 to remove the waste from the mortises.

**6** Turn the back legs over and transfer the back leg template (**B**) on to the wood pieces. Repeat previous procedures to remove the waste from the mortises. Lightly sand and stain the wood pieces with the exception of the seat wood piece which should only be stained on one side only. Once dry, polish the wood pieces with beeswax polish.

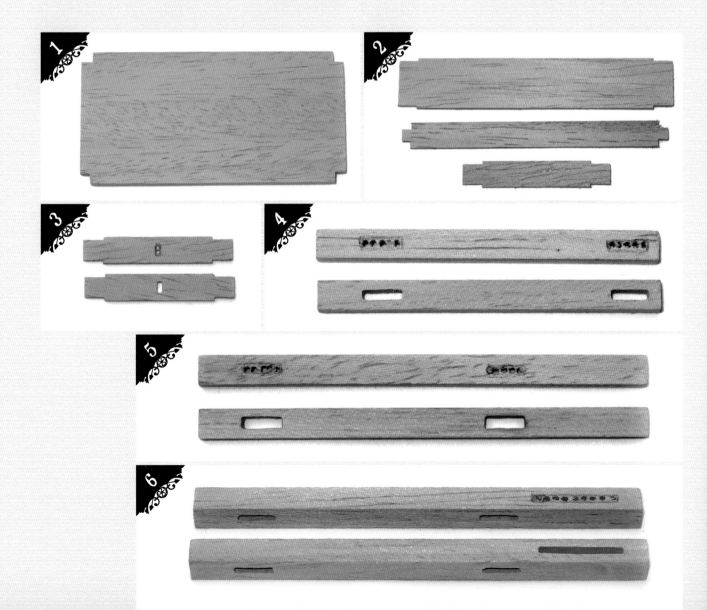

**7** Transfer the seat cover template on to a piece of paper. Roughly trim around the paper template and attach strips of low tack double-sided tape along the drawn lines on the underside of the paper and attach to the back of the leather.

**8** Use sharp scissors to cut out the shape. Carefully remove the paper template and adhesive tape from the back of the leather and glue the underside of the leather on to the unstained side and the

edges of the seat wood piece. All outside edges should be flush, so trim any excess leather using a sharp craft knife.

**9** Fit and glue a side stretcher and an arm wood piece in to the mortises in a back leg in the positions shown. Match up the tenons with the mortises in the front leg and secure into position. Make a mirror image of the construction with the remaining legs, side stretcher and arm pieces.

**10** Measure and mark 1⁵⁄₁₆in (33mm) from the end of each leg. Take the covered seat and fit between the front and back legs on one of the side constructions with the stained bottom edge of the seat flush with the marks. Fit the back and cross stretcher tenons into the positions shown and secure all pieces into position with a dab of glue.

**11** Carefully line up and secure the mortise and tenon joints with the remaining side construction and the underside of the seat with its position marks.

27

# ❧ Arts & Crafts Occasional Table ❧

S MALL AND LIGHTWEIGHT MULTI-FUNCTION
TABLES ARE THOUGHT TO HAVE
ORIGINATED AT THE BEGINNING OF THE
NINETEENTH CENTURY. THEIR ATTRACTION WAS
THAT THEY COULD BE MOVED AROUND A ROOM
AS REQUIRED, DEPENDING ON THEIR PURPOSE.
DURING THE EDWARDIAN ERA AN OCCASIONAL
TABLE IN THE HALLWAY MAY HAVE BEEN USED
TO HOLD THE POST WHICH WOULD HAVE BEEN
DELIVERED SEVERAL TIMES DURING THE DAY.

**Dimensions**  $2\frac{5}{32}$in (55mm) high; $1\frac{3}{4}$in (44mm) wide
**Skill level**  Intermediate
**Templates**  Page 155

## Why not try...

...piercing a heart decoration at the bottom of
each leg. See the hallstand project on page 16
step 8 for more information.

## MATERIALS & EQUIPMENT

♠ **From $\frac{3}{32}$in (2.5mm) thick obechi sheet
wood:**

– $1\frac{3}{4}$ x $1\frac{3}{4}$in (44 x 44mm) for top

– Four $2\frac{1}{16}$ x $\frac{13}{32}$in (52 x 10.5mm) for legs

– Four $1\frac{3}{4}$ x $\frac{3}{16}$in (44 x 5mm) for stretchers

♠ Oak wood stain

♠ Beeswax polish

♠ Tacky glue

# MAKING THE ARTS & CRAFTS OCCASIONAL TABLE

**1** Transfer the top template on to the top wood piece and cut out. Smooth the edge of the disc firstly using medium-grade sandpaper, followed by fine-grade sandpaper.

**2** Transfer the leg template (**A**) on to the leg wood pieces. Use a pin vice with a ¹⁄₁₆in (1.5mm) drill bit to drill a hole through the wood at each end of the rectangle.

**3** Use a sharp craft knife to remove the waste in between the drilled holes. Sand the opening smooth and to size using either a needle file or a folded piece of sandpaper.

**4** Transfer the leg template (**B**) on to the wood pieces and cut out. **TIP** To avoid the wood splitting at the tops of the legs repeat the procedures at steps 2 and 3 to remove the waste section.

**5** Transfer the lower stretcher template on to **two** stretcher pieces. Make a groove in the wood ³⁄₁₆in (5mm) wide and ³⁄₆₄in (1.25mm) deep by scoring along the marked lines and then using a needle file to make a channel in between the scored lines.

**6** Transfer the upper stretcher template on to the remaining stretcher wood pieces and cut them out. Apply oak wood stain to each of the wood pieces – sparingly to prevent the wood warping. Once they are dry, polish the wood pieces with beeswax polish. **TIP** Place the delicate pieces on a flat surface while they are being polished to avoid them splitting.

**7** Slot the lower stretchers and upper stretcher together and fix using a dab of tacky glue. Position and glue the stretchers into the slots in the legs, insetting the legs slightly inwards in the upper stretchers to allow the legs to splay outwards. Position and glue the top centrally on to the construction.

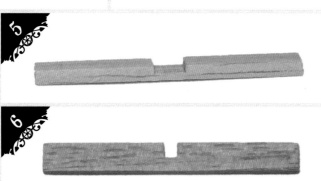

Craftsman dining table ~ page 34

Craftsman dining chair ~ page 36

# THE DINING ROOM

# IN THE DINING ROOM

IN MANY OF THE NEWLY BUILT suburban and garden city homes the dining room was situated at the front of the house. For the aspiring middle classes, a separate dining room suggested success as previously a room may have had to double as a living room and dining area. The room was used daily and even sharing an evening meal with the family was considered a special occasion.

Entertaining was important to the Edwardians and dining room interior decoration and furnishings were chosen to impress visitors. Reproduction furniture was favoured, and companies produced suites of dining furniture, with Chippendale and Sheraton styles being particularly popular. Strong, dark, masculine colour schemes complemented the rich polished furniture. Dark internal wood work still remained popular in the dining room.

In homes that favoured the Edwardian's passion for lighter and airier interiors, the simple unpretentious mood of the Arts & Crafts style prevailed. Walls were decorated in muddy natural colours, and shades of blues, green, red, brown and gold were fashionable. Wood work was painted in white, off-white or pale cream and dining furniture was made from oak using simple straight lines.

Wallpaper was the most approved choice of wall covering and there were a wide range of styles and patterns available at reasonable cost. Naturalistic themes such as flowers, foliage and animals were common and influenced by the Arts & Crafts movement and Art Nouveau style. Walls were generally papered up to the picture rail, and the area above up to the cornice was either painted to match the ceiling or covered with a frieze.

Hygiene was very important to the Edwardians and fitted carpets were considered unhygienic. Floorboards were exposed and stained in dark colours and then waxed. Rugs and carpet squares that were easily removable for cleaning partially covered wooden floors and they were patterned in the predominating current styles and oriental designs.

The heavily adorned window coverings of the Victorian era were also regarded as unhealthy dust traps. Simple window treatments of a roller blind and curtains, with a pelmet covering the rail became common. Patterned curtain fabrics often matched the wallpaper in the room.

An overhead rise and fall pendant lamp was the standard form of lighting in the dining room at the turn of the century. Shade designs varied and were generally made from silk, glass or beads. Wall lights were also popular and provided a softer and less direct light for diners.

# ❧ Craftsman Dining Table ❧

The American Arts & Crafts movement promoted architectural reform to provide honest, simple and affordable houses for the growing numbers of affluent middle-class people at the beginning of the twentieth century. Victorian residences were considered formal and oppressive so Craftsman bungalow-style homes were built outside the cities to provide a more open and airier layout for the family home. Period publications encouraged furnishing contemporary homes with fashionable Craftsman-style furniture.

**Dimensions** 2½in (64mm) high; 5½in (140mm) wide; 3in (76mm) deep
**Skill level** Intermediate
**Templates** Page 156

# MATERIALS & EQUIPMENT

♠ **From ³⁄₁₆in (5mm) thick obechi sheet wood:**
– Two 2⅞ x ⁵⁄₁₆in (73 x 8mm) for top stretchers

♠ **From ⅛in (3mm) thick obechi sheet wood:**
– Two 2⁷⁄₃₂ x ½in (56.5 x 13mm) for side stretchers
– Four 5½ x ¾in (140 x 19mm) for top slats

♠ **From ³⁄₃₂in (2.5mm) thick obechi sheet wood:**
– 4⅛ x ³⁄₈in (105 x 10mm) for cross stretcher

♠ **From ¼ x ¼in (6 x 6mm) obechi strip wood:**
– Four 2³⁄₁₆in (56mm) lengths for legs

♠ Dark oak wood stain

♠ Beeswax polish

♠ Tacky glue

# MAKING THE CRAFTSMAN DINING TABLE

**1** Take a top stretcher and, on the wide side of the wood, measure and mark ¼in (6mm) inwards from each end. Measure and mark ³⁄₃₂in (2.5mm) on the narrow edges of the wood piece at each end and join the pencil marks as shown. Remove the waste sections by chamfering (page 178) the wood at each end. Repeat the procedure with the other top stretcher.

**2** Transfer the side stretcher (**A**) and cross stretcher templates on to the corresponding wood pieces and cut out the shoulders and form the tenons. To prevent the wood splitting, first cut against the grain, using either mitre cutters or a craft knife, and then cut with the grain of the wood.

**3** Take the side stretcher wood pieces and transfer the side stretcher (**B**) template on to the two wood pieces. Use a pin vice with a ¹⁄₁₆in (1.5mm) drill bit to drill a series of holes through the wood within the drawn rectangle. Use a sharp craft

knife to remove the waste and sand the openings smooth and to size using a needle file.

**4** Take the leg pieces and transfer the leg template on to the four wood pieces. Repeat the procedure at step 3 using a ³⁄₃₂in (2.5mm) drill bit.

**5** Lightly sand and stain the wood pieces. Once dry, take the top slats and glue the long edges together to form the table top. Polish one side and the edges of

the table top with beeswax polish, together with the remaining dining table wood pieces.

**6** Fit and glue the side stretchers into the mortises in the legs and the cross stretcher into the mortises in the side stretchers. Glue the tops of the legs centrally on to the wide chamfered side of the top stretchers and position and glue the construction centrally on to the unpolished side of the table top.

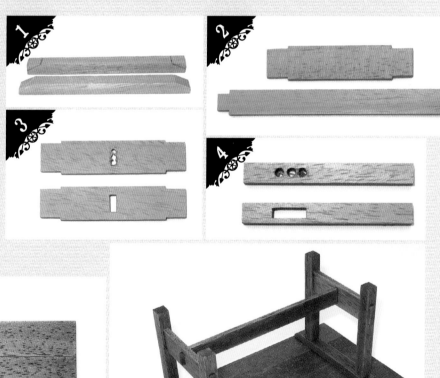

# Craftsman Dining Chair

I N RESPONSE TO THE SWELLING NUMBERS OF MIDDLE-CLASS CITIZENS IN AMERICA AT THE TURN OF THE CENTURY AND THEIR DESIRE FOR 'MODERN' HOMES, SEARS, ROEBUCK AND COMPANY – AN AMERICAN MAIL-ORDER RETAIL FIRM – PRODUCED AFFORDABLE, HIGH-QUALITY, PRE-CUT AND INDUSTRIALLY PRE-FABRICATED HOUSES. THEY SOLD THESE FLAT-PACKED BY MAIL ORDER FOR PEOPLE TO BUILD THEMSELVES. CRAFTSMAN-STYLE FURNITURE OR THE COMPANY'S OWN MAIL-ORDER FURNITURE AND HOMEWARE RANGES PERFECTLY COMPLEMENTED THESE NEW STYLES OF HOMES.

**Dimensions** 3¼in (83mm) high; 1½in (38mm) wide; 1⁷⁄₁₆in (37mm) deep

**Skill level** Intermediate

**Templates** Page 156

# MATERIALS & EQUIPMENT

♠ **From ³⁄₁₆in (5mm) thick obechi sheet wood:**

– 1⁷⁄₁₆ x 1³⁄₈in (37 x 35mm) for seat

♠ **From ³⁄₃₂in (2.5mm) thick obechi sheet wood:**

– Two ⁹⁄₁₆ x ³⁄₈in (14 x 10mm) for spacers

♠ **From ¼ x ⅛in (6 x 3mm) obechi strip wood:**

– Three 1¼in (32mm) lengths for back and front rails

♠ **From ⅛ x ⅛in (3 x 3mm) obechi strip wood:**

– Two 1¹⁷⁄₃₂in (39mm) lengths for front legs

– Two 3¼in (83mm) lengths for back legs

– Four 13⁄16in (30mm) lengths for side rails

– 1¼in (32mm) length for back bar

♠ **From ⅛ x ³⁄₃₂in (3 x 2.5mm) obechi strip wood:**

– Five 1in (25mm) lengths for back slats

♠ 2 x 2in (51 x 51mm) piece of fine glove leather for seat cover

♠ Paper for seat cover template

♠ Low tack double-sided tape

♠ Wood stain

♠ Beeswax polish

♠ Tacky glue

# MAKING THE CRAFTSMAN DINING CHAIR

**1** Lightly sand and stain each of the wood pieces. Stain one side only of the seat piece and do not stain the spacers. Polish each of the pieces with beeswax polish. Take a front and back leg and position opposite each other in a right-angled gluing jig. Position the spacer flat in the jig at the bottom of the legs. Position and glue a side rail between the legs, resting against the long edge of the spacer. Position another spacer lengthways against the previously positioned side rail and fix another side rail immediately above. Repeat with the other front and back leg as a mirror image. **TIP** Use a right-angled gluing jig at each stage to ensure the construction dries square.

**2** Turn the two constructions to rest on a back leg. Take a back rail and position and glue wide side down and 1/16in (1.5mm) from the tops of the legs. Position and glue the back slats below, wide side down and equidistant apart followed by the back bar. Rest another back rail, wide side down, against the short edge of the spacer at the bottom of the legs as shown and glue into place.

**3** Transfer the seat template on to the seat wood piece and cut out. To avoid the wood splitting, first cut against the grain using mitre cutters or a craft knife and then cut with the grain of the wood.

**4** Transfer the seat cover template on to a piece of paper. Roughly trim around the paper template and attach strips of low tack double-sided tape along the drawn lines on the underside of the paper and attach to the back of the leather.

**5** Use sharp scissors to cut out the shape. Carefully remove the paper template and adhesive tape from the back of the leather and glue the underside of the leather on to the unstained side and the edges of the seat wood piece. All outside edges should be flush; trim any excess leather using a sharp craft knife.

**6** Take the covered seat and fit and glue between the front and back legs, leaving a gap of 1/32in (1mm) from the tops of the front legs to the top of the seat. Position and glue the remaining front rail between the two front legs using the spacer's short edge for its position. Repeat the procedures to make a set of dining chairs.

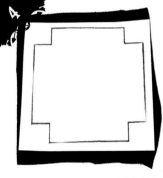

# ⚜ Craftsman Serving Table ⚜

**I**N LARGE DINING ROOMS, SERVING TABLES WERE OFTEN USED IN ADDITION TO A SIDEBOARD, BUT IN NEWLY BUILT SMALLER HOMES, A SERVING TABLE MAY HAVE BEEN USED INSTEAD OF A SIDEBOARD. IN AMERICA, AMMONIA FUMING WAS COMMONLY USED TO TREAT CRAFTSMAN-STYLE FURNITURE MADE FROM OAK. THE TANNIC ACID IN THE WOOD REACTED WITH THE AMMONIA TO PRODUCE VAPOURS THAT CAUSED EXPOSED WOOD TO PERMANENTLY DARKEN IN COLOUR, ENRICHING AND ENHANCING THE NATURAL BEAUTY OF THE WOOD.

**Dimensions** 3¹¹⁄₃₂in (85mm) high; 3⁹⁄₁₆in (90mm) wide; 1⅜in (35mm) deep

**Skill level** Intermediate

**Template** Page 156

# MATERIALS & EQUIPMENT

♠ **From ³⁄₁₆in (5mm) thick obechi wood:**

— 2¹⁵⁄₁₆ x ³¹⁄₆₄in (75 x 12.5mm) for back

♠ **From ⅛in (3mm) thick obechi wood:**

— Two ⅞ x ¾in (22 x 19mm) for sides

— Two ⅞ x ⁵⁄₁₆in (22 x 8mm) for side stretchers

♠ **From ³⁄₃₂in (2.5mm) thick obechi wood:**

— 2¹⁵⁄₁₆ x 1in (75 x 25mm) for drawer support

— 3⁹⁄₁₆ x 1⅜in (90 x 35mm) for top

— 3⁵⁄₁₆ x ¼in (84 x 6mm) for backrest

♠ **From ¹⁄₁₆in (1.5mm) thick obechi wood:**

— 3³⁄₁₆ x 1¹⁄₁₆in (81 x 27mm) for shelf

— Four 1¹¹⁄₃₂ x ⁵⁄₁₆in (34 x 8mm) for drawer back and front

— Four ⅞ x ⁵⁄₁₆in (22 x 8mm) for drawer sides

— Two 1⁷⁄₃₂ x ⅞in (31 x 22mm) for drawer bases

— Three 1 x ²¹⁄₆₄in (25 x 8.5mm) for drawer dividers – grain to run with short length

— 2¹⁵⁄₁₆ x 1in (75 x 25mm) for partition

♠ **From ³⁄₁₆ x ³⁄₁₆in (5 x 5mm) obechi strip wood:**

— Four 3in (76mm) lengths for legs

♠ Two brass drawer handle pulls

♠ Dark oak wood stain

♠ Beeswax polish

♠ Tacky glue

# MAKING THE CRAFTSMAN SERVING TABLE

1 Transfer the shelf template on to the shelf wood piece and cut out. To avoid the wood splitting, first cut against the grain of the wood using mitre cutters or a craft knife and then with the grain of the wood.

2 Lightly sand and stain the wood pieces. Position and glue a drawer front, back and two sides on to the outside edges of a drawer base wood piece. Repeat the procedure with the remaining drawer pieces.

3 Take two legs and position a side piece wide-side down in between. The top of the side piece should be flush with the tops of the legs. Take a side stretcher piece and position wide-side down and glue ⅜in (10mm) from the ends of the legs. Repeat the procedure with the remaining legs, side and side stretcher pieces.

4 Place the side constructions to rest on a leg with the side where pieces are inset facing outwards. Position and glue the back piece in between and wide-side down with the top edge flush with the tops of the legs. Position and glue the shelf to rest on top of the side stretchers with the cut-out sections resting against the back legs.

5 Take the drawer dividers and position and glue, with the narrow edge down, on top of the drawer support, one at each end and one centrally. Position and glue the partition piece on top. All outside edges are flush.

TIP Position the drawers inside the construction to help with the fit of the central drawer divider and remove whilst the glue dries.

6 Position and glue the construction to rest against the back piece. The partition side is positioned at the top of the frame and is flush with the tops of the legs.

7 Glue the top piece into place, so the back edge is flush with the back of the construction and the front and sides overlap equally. Stand and glue the backrest centrally on top of the table with the back flush with the back of the table. Polish the construction and drawer fronts with beeswax polish. Glue the drawer handle pulls on to the drawer fronts and insert the drawers into the table.

# ⚜ Bowls & Stands ⚜

Followers of the Arts & Crafts movement and Art Nouveau progressives believed everything in the home should have visual appeal as well as being functional. Elegant but useful bowls and stands were popular, often with botanically themed motifs and designs made in metalware, glass and ceramic. Surfaces in the dining room were much less overloaded than they were in Victorian times following the Edwardians' aversion to clutter.

**Skill level**  Beginner

# Materials & Equipment

## General Materials

♠ Super glue gel

♠ Circle paper punches: ⅛ and 1/16in (3 and 1.5mm) diameter

## For the Bonbon Stand

♠ ⅜in (10mm) silver-plated, fluted bead cap for dish

♠ 3/32in (2.5mm) nickel eyelet for stand

♠ **From pewter embossing sheet:**

– 1/16in (1.5mm) diameter round disc for filler

## For the Fruit Bowl

♠ 1 x 5/16in (25 x 8mm) gold-plated dish for bowl

♠ 1⅜ x 1in (35 x 25mm) gold-plated leaf finding for base

♠ **From brass embossing sheet:**

– ⅛in (3mm) diameter round disc for filler

♠ Copper spray paint and dark brown, spirit-based wood stain

## For the Pedestal Cake Stand

♠ 13/16in (21mm) gold-plated, fluted cap for plate

♠ ⅛in (3mm) brass eyelet for stand

♠ **From brass embossing sheet:**

– ⅛in (3mm) diameter round disc for filler

♠ White spray paint

♠ 3D gloss varnish

## For the Trivet

♠ ⅝in (16mm) square, antique gold-plated filigree for base

♠ Four 1/16in (1.5mm) antique brass eyelets for feet

# MAKING THE BONBON STAND

Position and glue the upturned dish to rest centrally on top of the narrow end of the eyelet stand using super glue gel. Position and glue the filler disc on top of the hole in the centre of the dish.

# MAKING THE FRUIT BOWL

Repeat the procedures for making the Bonbon Stand to make the Fruit Bowl, altering the eyelet stand for the leaf base. Apply several coats of copper spray paint, allowing each one to dry before applying the next. Once dry, create a patina by lightly covering all of the Fruit Bowl with a dark brown, spirit-based wood stain and allow it to settle in the grooved areas on the findings to highlight their design.

# MAKING THE PEDESTAL CAKE STAND

Repeat the procedures for making the Bonbon Stand to make the Pedestal Cake Stand. Apply several coats of white spray paint to cover the stand allowing each one to dry before applying the next. Carefully cover the cake stand with 3D gloss varnish to create a porcelain effect.

# MAKING THE TRIVET

Place the filigree base to rest top-side down. Position and glue the narrow end of the eyelet feet on to each corner of the base and once dry turn the Trivet and position the feet down.

# ❧ Reception Room Fireplace ❧

During the Edwardian era all reception rooms were heated with a coal fire. The fireplace would have been the focal point of the room and wooden surrounds with cast-iron grates and tiled cheeks were fashionable at this time. Surrounds were generally painted white or cream or left uncoloured and waxed. Individual patterned tiles or panels of tiles with Art Nouveau or Arts & Crafts designs were in vogue.

**Dimensions** $3^{31}/_{32}$in (101mm) high; $3^{5}/_{8}$in (92mm) wide; 2in (51mm) deep. To fit in opening $2^{13}/_{16}$in (71mm) high; $2^{9}/_{16}$in (65mm) wide; 1in (25mm) deep
**Skill level** Advanced
**Templates** Pages 157 and 158

# MATERIALS & EQUIPMENT

♠ **From $^{1}/_{8}$in (3mm) thick obechi sheet wood:**
– $2^{3}/_{4}$ x 1in (70 x 25mm) for lintel
– Two $3^{7}/_{8}$ x $^{3}/_{8}$in (98 x 10mm) for pilasters
– Two $^{3}/_{8}$ x $^{3}/_{8}$in (10 x 10mm) mantel feet

♠ **From $^{3}/_{32}$in (2.5mm) thick obechi sheet wood:**
– $3^{5}/_{8}$ x $^{1}/_{2}$in (92 x 13mm) for mantel shelf

♠ **From $^{1}/_{16}$in (1.5mm) thick obechi wood:**
– Two $2^{5}/_{8}$ x $^{1}/_{16}$in (66 x 1.5mm) for frame sides
– $1^{3}/_{8}$ x $^{1}/_{4}$in (35 x 6mm) for frame base

♠ **From $^{1}/_{8}$ x $^{1}/_{16}$in (3 x 1.5mm) obechi strip wood:**
– Two $2^{7}/_{8}$in (73mm) lengths for side trim
– $2^{3}/_{4}$in (70mm) length for top trim
– $1^{1}/_{2}$in (38mm) length for frame top

♠ **From $^{5}/_{16}$ x $^{3}/_{32}$in (8 x 2.5mm) grooved wood moulding:**
– Two $3^{1}/_{2}$in (88mm) lengths for pilaster decoration

♠ **From $^{1}/_{4}$ x $^{1}/_{16}$in (6 x 1.5mm) chamfered architrave moulding:**
– $3^{1}/_{4}$in (83mm) length for hearth front
– Two $^{3}/_{4}$in (19mm) lengths for hearth sides

♠ **From $^{3}/_{64}$in (1mm) thick cord:**
– $2^{3}/_{8}$in (60mm) length for beading

♠ **From 26-gauge (0.45mm) paper floral wire:**
– Seventeen $^{5}/_{8}$in (16mm) lengths for grate base bars
– Twenty one $^{17}/_{32}$in (13mm) lengths for grate front bars

♠ Ten $^{1}/_{2}$ x $^{1}/_{2}$in (13 x 13mm) wall tiles

♠ 1¹¹⁄₁₆ x ⁹⁄₁₆in (43 x 14mm) gold-plated filigree for lintel embellishment

♠ ⁹⁄₁₆ x ½in (14 x 13mm) gold-plated filigree for hood embellishment

♠ Sequin pin for grate handle

♠ Metal primer paint

♠ Black satin spray paint

♠ White or cream & grey acrylic paint

♠ A4 sheet of craft card

♠ Tacky glue

♠ HB pencil for graphite effect

# MAKING THE RECEPTION ROOM FIREPLACE

**1** Take the mantel shelf wood piece and round the corners on one long side using fine-grade sandpaper. Lightly sand the remaining wood pieces.

**2** Position and glue the lintel wood piece between the two pilasters. All pieces should be positioned wide-side down and the top edge of the lintel should be flush with the tops of the pilasters. Apply metal primer paint to the filigree embellishments and once dry, position and glue the lintel embellishment centrally on to the lintel.

**3** Position the pilaster decoration wood pieces centrally on top of the pilasters with one end flush with the top of the construction. Immediately below, position the mantel feet with the grain of wood pieces running vertically. Position the mantel shelf on top of the wooden surround with the straight back edge flush with the back of the construction and the ends overlapping equally on each side. Glue the pieces into position.

**4** Paint the fire surround with white or cream acrylic paint. Once dry, very lightly sand the painted wooden surface to smooth the finish of the paint. If necessary, re-paint and repeat the procedure if too much paint comes off. Buff the surround to produce a dull sheen using a piece of kitchen paper towel. **TIP** Take care when buffing the mantel embellishment to avoid removing the primer and paint. ☞

5 Transfer the fireplace templates on to the craft card. Score along the dotted lines using a craft knife and ruler and then cut out using the same tools. Take the front card piece and open out and fold as shown.

6 Take the back card piece and fold with the scored lines facing backwards. Attach the flaps on the back piece to the front card piece. The outside edges of the front's flaps sit neatly against the folds in the back card piece. All top and bottom edges are flush.

7 Take the side trim wood pieces and mitre (page 178) one end on each to an angle of 45 degrees using mitre cutters or a mitre block and

saw. Take the top trim wood piece and mitre each end to an angle of 45 degrees as shown.

8 Position and glue the trim wood pieces on top of the fire front as shown. The inside edge of the wood pieces should be flush with the scored lines and top opening. Position and glue the beading cord on top of the marked lines and across the back inside the opening.

9 Take the grate base card piece and position with the scored lines facing downwards. Take the grate base wire bars and position as

shown. Lay the remaining bars equidistant apart, trimming the ends of the wire placed in the corners for a neat fit. Glue the bars into place.

10 Take the grate front card piece and position with the scored lines facing downwards. Take the grate front wire bars and position as shown with the end bars sitting in the folds. Lay the remaining bars equidistant apart and glue into place.

11 Take the hood card piece and position with the scored lines facing forwards and the sides folded inwards. Place the frame top wood

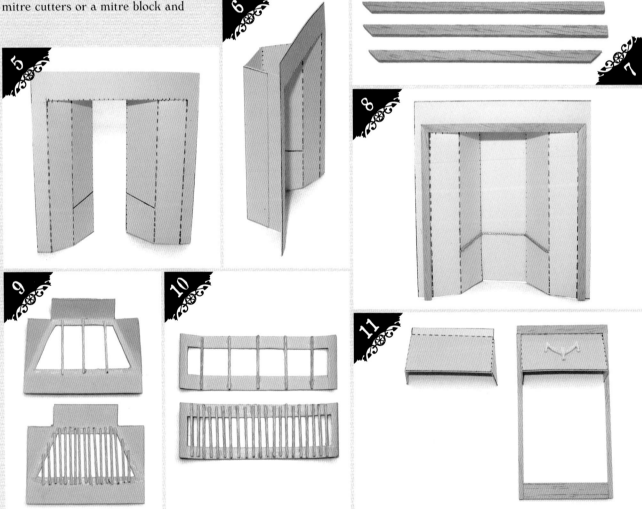

piece on top of the flap above the hood. The frame side wood pieces fit immediately below each end of the frame top piece and the frame base wood piece in between at the opposite end. Glue the pieces together and fix the hood embellishment in place. **TIP** Trim the loops off the top of the filigree embellishment using wire cutters.

**12** Position the grate base into the bottom of the opening and secure by gluing the flaps to the inside of the fireplace. Then position the hood construction on top of the fireplace as shown and glue in place. **TIP** To check the fit of the hood construction, slide a tile along the cheeks on each side.

**13** Take the ashtray front card piece and make a small hole centrally with a pin. With the scored lines facing outwards fold and glue

the end flaps on to the frame base. Trim the grate handle pin to measure ³⁄₁₆in (5mm) long, leaving ¹⁄₁₆in (1.5mm) of the head of the pin protruding, and glue into the hole.

**14** Position and glue the ashtray top card piece on top of the ashtray front. Secure the grate front on top of the ashtray with the side flaps resting on the inside of the side frame pieces as shown.

**15** Take the hearth card template and stand the hearth front and side wood pieces on top of the hearth. Chamfer (page 178) each end of the front wood piece and one end on each of the side pieces, then fit and glue the wood pieces on top of the card as shown.

**16** Lightly spray paint the register grate, hearth and two tile support cards with black spray paint several times. Once dry, use shades of grey acrylic paint to dry brush the back of the fireplace. Carefully shave some lead off a pencil using a craft knife. Use either a finger or paintbrush to rub the lead over the sprayed card constructions and tile supports to create a leaded effect.

**17** Position and glue the tiles on to the fireplace cheeks starting at the top. Position and glue a tile support card piece immediately below each row of tiles, trimming if necessary for a good fit. Place the wooden surround on top of the fireplace and stand and glue on top of the hearth.

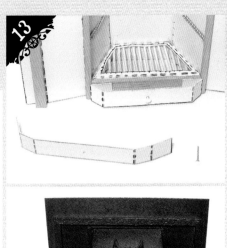

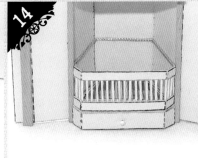

# ❧ Over-mantel Mirror ❧

T HE EDWARDIANS CONSIDERED THE FIREPLACE TO BE THE FOCAL POINT OF THE ROOM AND ONE OF ITS DOMINANT FEATURES IN A RECEPTION ROOM WOULD HAVE BEEN AN OVER-MANTEL MIRROR EITHER INCORPORATED INTO THE WOODEN FIRE SURROUND OR MADE INDIVIDUALLY AND LOCATED ON TOP OF THE MANTEL SHELF. THESE MIRRORS WERE OFTEN VERY LARGE AND ON OCCASIONS NEARLY AS HIGH AS THE PICTURE RAIL.

**Dimensions**  2⅜in (60mm) high; 3⁷⁄₁₆in (87mm) wide; ⁵⁄₁₆in (8mm) deep
**Skill level**  Beginner

# MATERIALS & EQUIPMENT

♠ **From ¹⁄₁₆in (1.5mm) thick obechi sheet wood:**
– 3⁷⁄₁₆ x ⁵⁄₁₆in (87 x 8mm) for shelf
– 2¹³⁄₁₆ x ⁵⁄₁₆in (71 x 8mm) for top panel
– 2¹³⁄₁₆ x ³⁄₁₆in (71 x 5mm) for bottom panel
– 3¼ x ¼in (82 x 6mm) for base
– Two 1¾ x ³⁄₁₆in (44 x 5mm) for vertical panels

♠ **From ¹⁄₃₂in (1mm) thick obechi sheet wood:**
– 3 x 2¼in (76 x 57mm) for back

♠ **From ³⁄₁₆ x ³⁄₁₆in (5 x 5mm) obechi strip wood:**
– Two 2¼in (57mm) lengths for sides

♠ **From ³⁄₆₄in (1mm) plastic sheet mirror:**
– 3 x 2¼in (76 x 57mm) for mirror

♠ White or cream acrylic paint

♠ Tacky glue

# MAKING THE OVER-MANTEL MIRROR

1 Take the side pieces and measure and mark ³⁄₃₂in (2.5mm) inwards from a long outside edge. Turn the wood pieces over and repeat the procedure. Use a craft knife and metal ruler to cut half way down into the wood pieces along the marked lines to remove a ³⁄₃₂in (2.5mm) by ³⁄₃₂in (2.5mm) section and create a rebate (page 178) in each of the wood pieces.

2 Take the shelf wood piece and round the corners on one long side using fine-grade sandpaper. Lightly sand the wooden components and paint them sparingly to avoid warping. Paint one side only of the back piece. Once dry, very lightly sand all sides of the painted surfaces to smooth the finish. If necessary, re-paint and repeat the procedure if too much paint comes off. Buff the pieces to produce a dull sheen using a piece of kitchen paper towel.

3 Position and glue the unpainted side of the back wood piece on to the back of the mirror. Position the side pieces with the rebate sections facing upwards and carefully glue the narrow outside edges of the mirror inside the rebates.
**TIP** Ensure that the plastic protective covering has been removed from the mirror and only a small amount of glue is used, to avoid it seeping through the side edges.

4 Carefully glue the top panel on top of the mirror at one end, ensuring that the outside edge is flush with the outside edge of the mirror. Position and glue the shelf to rest on top with the straight back edge flush with the back of the mirror and the ends overlapping the mirror equally.

5 Following the procedures at step 4, position and glue the bottom panel and base piece on to the opposite end of the mirror. The two vertical panels should be positioned and carefully glued on top of the mirror leaving a gap of ¹³⁄₁₆in (20mm) between each.

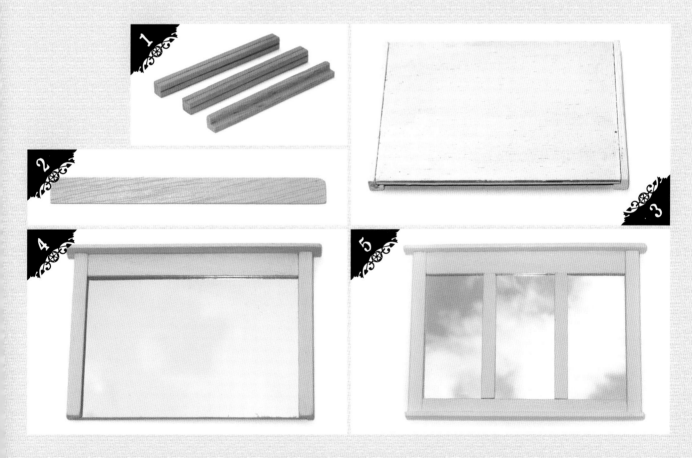

# ❧ Vase of Roses ❧

**V**ASES AND BOWLS OF FLOWERS WERE USED THROUGHOUT THE HOUSE DURING EDWARDIAN TIMES AND PUBLICATIONS ENCOURAGED SIMPLE AND NATURALISTIC FLORAL DISPLAYS. THE ROSE WAS A WIDESPREAD ART NOUVEAU MOTIF AND IT WAS TRANSLATED ON TO TILES, WALLPAPER, FABRICS AND RUGS – USUALLY IN A STYLIZED FORM. ROSES WERE PRESENTED AS A CENTREPIECE FOR THE DINING TABLE ARRANGED IN SILVER TRUMPET-SHAPED VASES, OR POSIES WERE ALSO CONSIDERED HIGHLY TASTEFUL.

**Dimensions** 1¼in (32mm) high; ⅞in (22mm) wide
**Skill level** Beginner

# MATERIALS & EQUIPMENT

♠ **From red paper ribbon:**

– Seventy five ³⁄₁₆in (5mm) discs for petals

♠ **From leaf green paper ribbon:**

– Three ⁵⁄₁₆in (8mm) diameter daisy shapes for calyx

♠ **From 26-gauge (0.45mm) green paper covered wire:**

– Three 1in (25mm) lengths for stems

♠ ³⁄₁₆in (5mm) diameter circle paper punch

♠ ⁵⁄₁₆in (8mm) daisy paper punch

♠ Etched brass rose leaves

♠ ¹¹⁄₁₆ x ¹¹⁄₃₂in (17 x 9mm) silver-plated cone bead for vase

♠ ⅜in (10mm) silver-plated bead cap for vase base

♠ Metal primer paint

♠ Leaf green acrylic paint

♠ Super glue gel

♠ Tacky glue

# MAKING THE VASE OF ROSES

1 Take a wire stem and dab a tiny amount of tacky glue on to one end. Roll one of the paper petal discs around the glue-covered stem to hide the end of the wire. Dab a tiny amount of tacky glue around the bottom edge of the previously glued paper petal and roll and secure a new petal into place. The centre of a new petal centrally covers the join in the previously positioned petal. **TIP** The creases in the paper petals should run in-line with the length of wire at each stage.

2 Continue to repeat the procedure to attach another twenty three paper petals, twisting the rose head in the same direction each time to ensure a uniform shape. Do not press the petals too tightly around the head of the rose. As the rose head grows and a new petal is attached it should slightly overlap the previously positioned petal. Once dry, ease the petals out for a fuller bloom using a finger nail or small tool.

3 Take the paper calyx and neatly trim off excess petals to create a calyx with five sepals. Pierce a small hole in the centre with a pin or fine drill bit and thread the calyx on to the end of the wire and up the stem. Arrange and glue the sepals equally around the bottom of the rose head.

4 Prime and then paint the metal rose leaves on both sides and once dry, trim off two sets of five leaves. Shape the leaves with the embossed side facing upwards and glue on to the side of the stem at the top with a dab of super glue gel. Glue the remaining leaves on the opposite side just slightly further down the stem.

5 Repeat the procedures to make two more roses. Glue the narrow end of the vase centrally on top of the domed base, using super glue gel, and arrange the roses inside. **TIP** If making more roses, use more or fewer petal discs to create different stages of bud.

Arts & Crafts
Corner Sofa
- page 54

Arts & Crafts
Reclining Armchair
- page 58

# THE LIVING ROOM

# IN THE LIVING ROOM

**T**HE LIVING ROOM WAS OFTEN situated at the back of newly built Edwardian homes overlooking the garden. Previously, Victorian drawing rooms were only used for receiving visitors and were generally crammed full of furniture and ornaments and decorated in dark, rich colours. The Edwardian drawing room was much less cluttered and decorated in lighter colours. Whilst still used as a reception room its other function was as a family living room, hence the change of name from drawing room to living room.

There was often a definite feminine influence in the decoration and furnishing of the living room and light-coloured chintz (rose and ribbon printed patterns in pale greens, pinks, blues and creams), wallpapers and soft furnishings were particularly popular. In living rooms not decorated in this way the Arts & Crafts movement and Art Nouveau style of decoration and furnishing were highly fashionable.

Like the dining room, walls were usually covered with patterned paper and a frieze, although the Arts & Crafts movement's trend for plain, light-coloured walls did become more popular towards the end of the era, with the only pattern on the wall from the frieze. Generally, light colours were used for decorating the living room and pale shades of green, blue, mauve and pink were often favoured.

Health and hygiene was a serious consideration and white, cream or off-white enamel-painted woodwork was popular as it could be easily cleaned. French windows opening out into the garden were the latest trend and followed the Edwardians' new respect for the outdoors and fresh air. The Edwardians also gradually introduced fitted furniture into their houses as it cut down on the areas where dust and dirt particles could settle and also helped to create a more spacious feel to the room.

Manufacturers of furniture produced suites and reproduction classical styles of living room furniture and Arts & Crafts designs were popular. Relaxing and comfortable upholstered chairs were chosen carefully to make sure the ambiance of the living room was tranquil and restful.

Walls were decorated with framed paintings, prints and photographs, often suspended on chains and hung from picture rails. Ornamental decoration included clocks, porcelain figures, glass vases and dishes, plates and decorative metalware. A piano or gramophone would generally be found in the living room as home entertainment was important to the Edwardians.

Living rooms were usually lit by either a pendant lamp hung from the ceiling or bracket wall lights. Standard or floor lamps were popular and also portable table and desk lamps. Shades were similar to those found in the hallway and dining room.

# ❧ Arts & Crafts Corner Sofa ❧

**W**ILLIAM MORRIS WAS ONE OF THE MOST INFLUENTIAL DESIGNERS AND EXPONENTS OF THE ARTS & CRAFTS MOVEMENT. HE SOUGHT TO RE-CAPTURE THE CRAFTSMANSHIP IN INTERIORS AND FURNISHINGS THAT HAD BEEN LOST TO INDUSTRIALISATION. DURING THE VICTORIAN ERA, HIS HAND-PRODUCED FURNITURE WOULD HAVE BEEN AFFORDED BY ONLY THE VERY WEALTHY. BY THE TURN OF THE CENTURY HIS IDEAS HAD BEEN COPIED AND PIECES BEGAN TO BE COMMERCIALLY PRODUCED LIKE THIS 'MORRIS-STYLE' CORNER SOFA.

**Dimensions** 4⅞in (124mm) wide; 3⁷⁄₃₂in (82mm) high; 2¼in (57mm) deep
**Skill level** Intermediate
**Templates** Page 159

# MATERIALS & EQUIPMENT

♠ **From ³⁄₁₆in (5mm) thick obechi wood:**
– 4¾ x 2⅛in (121 x 54mm) for back
– 2⅛ x 2in (54 x 51mm) for side – grain to run with short length
– 4⁹⁄₁₆ x 2in (116 x 51mm) for base

♠ **From ⅛in (3mm) thick obechi wood:**
– 4¹⁷⁄₃₂ x 1³¹⁄₃₂in (115 x 50mm) for seat cushion

♠ **From ³⁄₁₆ x ³⁄₁₆in (5 x 5mm) thick mahogany wood:**
– Four 1¼in (32mm) lengths for legs

♠ **From pale-coloured craft card:**
– 1¹⁵⁄₁₆ x 1¹¹⁄₁₆in (49 x 43mm) for side cushion
– 4½ x 1¹¹⁄₁₆in (114 x 43mm) for back cushion
– 7 x 2³⁄₃₂in (178 x 53mm) for back tidy

♠ **From Arts & Crafts-style printed patchwork fabric:**
– Two 6 x 3½in (152 x 89mm) for seat and back cushion covers – pattern to run with length
– 3½ x 3½in (89 x 89mm) for side cushion cover
– 8 x 3⅛in (203 x 80mm) for back tidy – pattern to run with length
– 8 x ½in (203 x 13mm) for trim – pattern to run with length

♠ **From 4oz (200g) wadding:**

− $4^{17}/_{32}$ x $1^{31}/_{32}$in (115 x 50mm) for seat cushion

− $1^{15}/_{16}$ x $1^{11}/_{16}$in (49 x 43mm) for side cushion

− $4^{1}/_{2}$ x $1^{11}/_{16}$in (114 x 43mm) for back cushion

♠ Mahogany wood stain

♠ Beeswax polish

♠ Tacky glue

# MAKING THE ARTS & CRAFTS CORNER SOFA

**1** Transfer the back template on to the back wood piece and cut out. To prevent the wood from splitting, first cut against the grain and then cut with the grain. Repeat the procedure with the side and base wood pieces.

**2** Take the back wood piece and stain the edge between the two cut-out sections with mahogany wood stain. Stain the shortest edge on the side wood piece and position the base piece as shown. Stain the side of the wood facing upwards.

**3** Polish the legs and the stained wooden parts with beeswax polish. Take the base wood piece and a leg, and position and glue together as shown. The top of the leg should be flush with the top of the base piece. **TIP** Use a right-angled gluing jig at each stage to ensure the construction dries square.

**4** Take the back wood piece and two legs and position and glue together as shown. Repeat the procedure with the side and remaining leg wood piece.

5 Position and glue the side and base constructions on top of the back section as shown. All outside edges are flush.

6 Take the seat cushion wood piece and round one long edge on one side only using fine-grade sandpaper. Repeat the procedure on the sofa's inside top back edge and the inside top and front edges on the side of the sofa.

7 Take the seat cushion wood piece and attach the seat cushion wadding using a smear of glue on to the side of the wood with the rounded edge. Mark the underside of the wood with an arrow to show the position of the rounded edge to indicate the front of the cushion for fabric orientation.

8 Place the seat cushion cover piece pattern face-down and position the cushion, wadding side down, centrally on top of the fabric. Roughly trim the corners off the fabric. Glue the opposite edges of the fabric neatly over on to the underside of the wood before gluing the remaining edges.

9 Attach the side cushion wadding to the side cushion card piece using a smear of glue and mark the underside with an arrow pointing to one long edge to indicate the top of the cushion for fabric orientation. Place the seat cushion fabric piece face down and position the side cushion, wadding side down, on top of the fabric.

10 Slide the card down the fabric leaving an overhang of fabric at the bottom and left-hand side of ¼in (6mm). Glue the fabric on the left-hand side to the back of the card.

11 Position the folded section in to the corner of the sofa as shown, with the top of the card, flush with the top edge of the sofa and glue into place. Neatly take the remaining fabric around the front and over the top of the side piece and secure the excess on the outside of the sofa. Spread and glue the fabric out wider at the top corner.

12 Attach the back cushion wadding to the back cushion card piece using a smear of glue and mark the underside with an arrow pointing to one long edge to indicate the top of the cushion. Position wadding side down on to the

underside of the back fabric allowing a small overhang of no more than ¼in (6mm) at the bottom and right-hand side. Glue the fabric to the back of the card on the right-hand side.

**13** Position the folded section in the corner of the sofa, with the top of the card flush with the top edge of the sofa. Neatly take the remaining fabric around the side and over the top of the back piece and secure the excess on to the outside of the sofa. Spread and glue the fabric out wider at the top corner.

**14** Take the trim fabric strip and position with the pattern face down. Fold one third of the fabric over widthways and lightly glue on to itself. Fold and glue enough of the remaining edge over to make a strip measuring ³⁄₁₆in (5mm) wide.

**15** Position and glue the fabric trim around the edge of the sofa's base, overlapping the ends around the side and back of the sofa. Trim any excess bulky fabric off the outside of the sofa.

**16** Take the back tidy card piece, and check it will neatly fit around the back of the sofa. Cover with the fabric following previous procedures, without wadding, bringing and gluing the excess fabric neatly around the back of the card. Position and glue around the outside of the sofa. Position and glue the seat cushion on top of the base.

# ❧ Arts & Crafts Reclining Armchair ❧

Previously, upholstered seating had been very upright and formal, and armchairs were now made for relaxation. William Morris was responsible for producing the innovative 'Morris adjustable chair', which introduced the concept of the reclining seat. 'Morris style' reclining armchairs were widely copied in Britain and America during the Edwardian era and provided up-to-the-minute style to any reception room.

**Dimensions**  3½in (89mm) high; 2⅜in (60mm) wide; 2¾in (70mm) deep
**Skill level**  Beginner

# MATERIALS & EQUIPMENT

♠ **From ³⁄₁₆in (5mm) thick mahogany sheet wood:**
– Two 1⅝ x ¼in (41 x 6mm) for side stretchers
– Four 1⅞ x ³⁄₁₆in (48 x 5mm) for legs
– 1¾ x 1⅝in (44 x 41mm) for base
– Two 1¾ x ¼in (44 x 6mm) for front and back stretchers

♠ **From ⅛in (3mm) thick mahogany sheet wood:**
– Eight ⅝ x ³⁄₁₆in (16 x 5mm) for side slats
– Two 2½ x ⁵⁄₁₆in (64 x 8mm) for arms
– Two 1⅜ x ³⁄₁₆in (34 x 5mm) for back rails
– Two 2¼ x ³⁄₁₆in (57 x 5mm) for back frame
– Three 1¾ x ³⁄₁₆in (44 x 5mm) for back slats

♠ **From ³⁄₁₆in (5mm) thick obechi sheet wood:**
– 1¾ x 1⅝in (44 x 41mm) for seat cushion

♠ **From ¹⁄₁₆in (1.5mm) thick obechi sheet wood:**
– 1¾ x 1⅝in (44 x 41mm) for back cushion

♠ **From 4oz (200g) weight wadding:**
– Two 1¾ x 1⅝in (44 x 41mm) for cushion wadding

♠ **From white or cream craft card:**
– 1¹¹⁄₁₆ x 1⁹⁄₁₆in (43 x 40mm) for back tidy

♠ **From Arts & Crafts-style printed patchwork fabric:**
– Two 3¼ x 3in (83 x 76mm) for cushion covers – pattern to run with the width
– 2¼ x 2⅛in (57 x 54mm) for back tidy cover – pattern to run with the width
♠ Tacky glue
♠ Beeswax polish

# MAKING THE ARTS & CRAFTS RECLINING ARMCHAIR

**1** Position a side stretcher wood piece wide side down between two legs and 1in (25mm) from one end of the legs. Take four side slats and position equidistant, wide side down, in the gap above. Join the pieces using tacky glue and repeat the procedure with the remaining legs, side stretcher and side slats. **TIP** Use a right-angled gluing jig at each stage.

**2** Take the base piece and the front and back stretchers. Stand the stretchers on their narrow edges and glue on to the base's long edges. All bottom edges of the construction are flush and from the top the base piece is inset.

**3** Place a side construction with the side where the slats are inset facing downwards. Take the base construction and position and glue an open edge on to the side construction, with the flush side of the base level with the top edge of the side stretcher.

**4** Place the remaining side construction with the side where the slats are inset facing downwards and repeat the procedure at step 3 to attach to the base.

**5** Take the arm pieces and shape one end on the wide side of the wood as shown. Position and glue on top of the legs and side slats with the rounded end facing upwards and protruding from the ends of the legs by 3/16in (5mm). The inside edge of the arms must be flush with the inside edges of the legs and side slats.

**6** Position the back rails between the back frame pieces. All pieces are positioned wide side down, and one end the construction is flush. At the other end, the back rail is inset by 1/8in (3mm). Position and glue the back slats wide side down and equidistant apart inside the construction. ☞

7 Polish the chair and back constructions with beeswax polish. Position and glue the back construction in between the arms at the back of the chair, with the straight narrow edge resting on top of the back stretcher and the top tilting outwards.

8 Take the seat cushion wood piece and attach the cushion wadding using a smear of glue. Place the cushion fabric piece, pattern face down, then position the cushion, wadding side down, centrally on top of the fabric.

Roughly trim the corners off the fabric. Note that the short edges of the fabric-covered wood are the top and bottom of the cushion.

9 Glue the opposite edges of the fabric neatly over on to the underside of the wood before gluing the remaining edges. Repeat the procedure with the back cushion wood piece, wadding and fabric. Note that the short edges of the fabric-covered wood are the top and bottom of the cushion.

10 Take the back tidy card piece and follow the procedures at steps 8 and 9, without wadding, to cover the card piece. Position and glue on to the back cushion wood piece to cover all untidy edges. Note that the short edges of the fabric and card are the top and bottom of the tidy.

11 Slide the seat cushion on to the seat of the chair. Place the back cushion on top and rest against the back of the chair. Repeat the procedure to make a matching pair of chairs.

# ❧ Arts & Crafts Lady's Writing Desk ❧

Small, elegant writing desks for ladies originated during the seventeenth century. A lady from the Edwardian era would have set time aside each day to sit at her desk to deal with daily correspondence. The introduction of picture postcards and half-penny stamps at the end of the nineteenth century created a huge increase in postal communication. Postcards that were posted in the morning would often arrive in the afternoon on the same day.

**Dimensions** 3⅛in (80mm) high; 2¹¹⁄₁₆in (68mm) wide; 1²³⁄₃₂in (44mm) deep

**Skill level** Beginner

**Templates** Page 160

# MATERIALS & EQUIPMENT

♠ **From ⅛in (3mm) thick obechi sheet wood:**
- Two 2¼ x ⅜in (57 x 10mm) for backs
- ½ x ⅜in (13 x 10mm) for compartment middle – grain to run with the short length

♠ **From ³⁄₃₂in (2.5mm) thick obechi sheet wood:**
- Two 1⅜ x ⅜in (35 x 10mm) for sides
- Two ⅜ x ⅜in (10 x 10mm) for compartment ends

♠ **From ¹⁄₁₆in (1.5mm) thick obechi sheet wood:**
- Two 2⁷⁄₃₂ x ²³⁄₆₄in (56 x 9mm) for drawer front and back
- 2⁷⁄₁₆ x 1⅝in (62 x 41mm) for drawer support
- 2¹¹⁄₁₆ x 1²³⁄₃₂in (68 x 44mm) for table top
- 2¹¹⁄₁₆ x ²³⁄₃₂in (68 x 18mm) for compartment top
- 2³⁄₃₂ x 1¹¹⁄₃₂in (53 x 34mm) for drawer base

- Two 1¹¹⁄₃₂ x ²³⁄₆₄in (34 x 9mm) for drawer sides
- Two ½ x ⅜in (13 x 10mm) for compartment dividers – grain to run with the short length
- Two ³⁄₁₆ x ³⁄₁₆in (5 x 5mm) for caps

♠ **From ⅛ x ⅛in (3 x 3mm) obechi strip wood:**
- Four 2⅜in (60mm) lengths for legs
- Four ⅜in (10mm) lengths for end pillars
- Two ³⁄₁₆in (5mm) lengths for top pillars

♠ Two ³⁄₃₂in (2.5mm) diameter brass drawer knobs

♠ Oak wood stain

♠ Beeswax polish

♠ Tacky glue

# MAKING THE ARTS & CRAFTS LADY'S WRITING DESK

**1** Transfer the desk drawer support template on to the drawer support wood piece and cut out. To avoid the wood splitting, first cut against the grain of the wood using either mitre cutters or a craft knife and then cut with the grain of the wood.

**2** Transfer the drill hole positions from the desk drawer front template on to the drawer front. Use a pin vice with a ¹⁄₁₆in (1.5mm) drill bit to drill holes through the wood. Lightly sand all of the wood pieces and stain sparingly to prevent the wood warping.

**3** Position and glue a side piece, wide-side down, between two legs. The top edge of the side piece should be flush with the tops of the legs. Repeat the procedure with the two remaining legs and side piece. **TIP** Use a right-angled gluing jig at each stage to ensure the construction dries square.

**4** Position and glue a back wood piece wide-side down between the two side constructions. The inset side on each of the leg constructions should face outwards and the top of the back piece should be flush with the tops of the legs.

**5** Slot the drawer support to rest against the bottom edges of the side and back pieces and glue into place. Take the table top wood piece and position and glue on top of the construction; one long edge is flush with the back of the construction and the sides and front overlap the edges equally.

**6** Glue the drawer knobs into the drawer front and then glue the drawer front and back and drawer sides on to the outside edges of the drawer base.

**7** Position and glue a compartment end piece between two end pillars. All outside edges should be flush and all grains should run in

line. Repeat the procedure with the remaining compartment end and two end pillars.

**8** Take a back piece and position the long edge down on the table top at the back leaving an equal gap at each end. Stand the end pillar constructions against each end of the back piece with the inset sides facing outwards. Check all pieces are flush with the back edge of the desk before gluing into place.

**9** Position and glue a short edge of the compartment middle against the back piece, leaving an equal opening on each side. Take the compartment dividers and position the short edges against the back and centrally in the two gaps. Glue the pieces into place.

**10** Position and glue the compartment top piece into position, with the back edge flush with the back of the construction, and the sides and front overlapping equally. Position and glue the top pillars on to the compartment top to run in line with the legs and back pillars. Glue the caps on top of the pillars with the grains running in line with the table top. Slide the drawer into position. Polish the desk with beeswax polish.

# Why not try...

...scanning and reducing some Edwardian photographs into miniature and gluing into small metal frames for display on the desk or shelves.

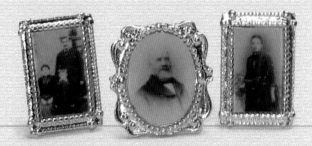

# ❧ Arts & Crafts Desk Chair ❧

T HERE HAVE BEEN MANY INFLUENCES
THAT HAVE CAUSED NEW FURNITURE
STYLES TO DEVELOP WITHIN EACH
PERIOD OF HISTORY. ALL STYLES HAVE THEIR
OWN DISTINCTIVE CHARACTERISTICS AND
IT IS PERHAPS THE CHAIR MORE THAN ANY
OTHER PIECE OF FURNITURE THAT IS CHOSEN
BY DESIGNERS TO ILLUSTRATE THEIR SKILLS
AND ORIGINALITY. THIS SIMPLE, RECTILINEAR
ARTS & CRAFTS CHAIR IS TYPICAL OF THE
MOVEMENT'S STYLE.

**Dimensions** 3⁵⁄₁₆in (84mm) high; 1⁷⁄₁₆in (37mm) wide;
1¹³⁄₃₂in (36mm) deep
**Skill level** Beginner
**Templates** Page 160

# MATERIALS & EQUIPMENT

♠ **From ¹⁄₁₆in (1.5mm) thick obechi wood:**

– 1⅜ x 1⅜in (35 x 35mm) for seat

– Two ³⁄₁₆ x ³⁄₁₆in (5 x 5mm) for caps

♠ **From ¼ x ⅛in (6 x 3mm) obechi
strip wood:**

– Five 1⅛in (29mm) lengths for rails

♠ **From ⅛ by ⅛in (3 x 3mm) obechi
strip wood:**

– Two 3¼in (82mm) lengths for back legs

– Two 1⅜in (35mm) lengths for front legs

– Seven 1⅛in (29mm) lengths for stretchers
and slats

♠ Oak wood stain

♠ Tacky glue

♠ Beeswax polish

# MAKING THE ARTS & CRAFTS DESK CHAIR

1 Position the seat wood piece with the wood grain running horizontally, then transfer the seat template on to the seat wood piece and cut out. To prevent the wood from splitting, first cut against the grain and then cut with the grain of the wood. Lightly sand all of the wood pieces and stain them sparingly to prevent warping.

2 Take a front and back leg, a rail and a stretcher and glue together as shown on the desk chair leg construction template. Repeat the procedure with the remaining front and back legs, a stretcher and a rail.

3 Place the constructions to rest on their back legs and glue a rail between and in line with the previously positioned rail pieces. Glue a rail ⅛in (3mm) down from the tops of the back legs.

4 Place a slat wood piece vertically and centrally below the top rail. Glue another slat on each side leaving a gap of ³⁄₁₆in (5mm) between each. Glue a slat horizontally and immediately below the previously positioned slats.

5 Position and glue a rail between the two front legs, in line with the previously positioned rails. Glue the remaining stretcher to fit centrally between the two stretchers at the bottom of the chair.

6 Glue the seat wood piece to rest on top of the rails and the caps on top of the two back legs with the grain of the wood pieces running in line with the grain in the seat and the edges overlapping the chair legs equally on each side. Polish the chair with beeswax polish.

# ⊰ Desk Accessories ⊱

**P**OSTAL COMMUNICATION INCREASED DURING THE EDWARDIAN ERA. DESK ACCESSORIES, WRITING EQUIPMENT AND POSTAL SUPPLIES BECAME INCREASINGLY POPULAR AND WERE READILY AVAILABLE. ALTHOUGH PRIMARILY FUNCTIONAL, THEY WERE ALSO OFTEN DECORATIVE, WITH DELICATE SETS OF ACCESSORIES AND EQUIPMENT BEING PRODUCED ESPECIALLY FOR THE EDWARDIAN LADY'S DESK. BOOKS AND MAGAZINE ARTICLES OF THE ERA PROVIDED ADVICE ON HOW TO DEAL WITH DAILY CORRESPONDENCE.

**Skill level** Beginner

# MATERIALS & EQUIPMENT

## GENERAL MATERIALS
- ♠ Wood stain
- ♠ Super glue gel
- ♠ Tacky glue

## FOR THE BELL
- ♠ 5/16in (8mm) gilt liberty bell
- ♠ 9/16in (14mm) wooden belaying pin for handle

## FOR THE CAPSTAN INKWELL
- ♠ 1/8in (3mm) gilt eyelet for base
- ♠ 5/16in (8mm) gold liberty bell clanger for lid

## FOR THE PEN WIPE
- ♠ 1/8in (3mm) gilt eyelet for base
- ♠ Small bundle of paint brush bristles

## FOR THE PEN
- ♠ 1in (25mm) length of 22-gauge (0.71mm) soft, silver-plated wire
- ♠ Black enamel paint

## FOR THE PENCIL
- ♠ 1in (25mm) length of straight 000 centre cane
- ♠ Black and silver acrylic paint

## FOR THE ROCKER BLOTTER
- ♠ **From 3/8in (10mm) diameter hardwood dowel:**
  - – 3/16in (5mm) length for rocker
  - – 3/8in (10mm) wooden double column for handle
- ♠ 1/2 x 3/16in (13 x 5mm) strip of grey paper for blotter

## FOR THE PAPERCLIP

♠ **From ¹⁄₃₂in (1mm) thick obechi wood:**

– ⁷⁄₁₆ by ⁵⁄₁₆in (11 x 8mm) for base

♠ ³⁄₈in (10mm) double column for disc

♠ ³⁄₈ x ¼in (10 x 6mm) metal filigree for clip

## FOR THE SEAL AND SEALING WAX

♠ ⁹⁄₁₆in (14mm) wooden belaying pin for handle

♠ ⁵⁄₆₄in (2mm) gold-plated cap for seal

♠ Dark red polymer clay for sealing wax

## FOR THE LETTER OPENER

♠ **From ¹⁄₃₂in (1mm) thick obechi wood:**

– Two ⁵⁄₈ x ³⁄₃₂in (16 x 2.5mm) for handle

♠ Small nickel brad for blade

## FOR THE MAGNIFYING GLASS

♠ ⁵⁄₁₆in (8mm) gold-plated jump ring for frame

♠ ⁹⁄₁₆in (14mm) wooden belaying pin for handle

♠ 3D gloss varnish

# MAKING THE BELL

Remove the clanger from the bell and retain for the capstan inkwell. Stain or paint the belaying pin and insert and glue the straight end into the top of the bell to make the handle.

# MAKING THE CAPSTAN INKWELL

Take the clanger from the bell and cut halfway across the small disc, as shown, using wire cutters. Hold the metal piece at one end and bend the section between the discs to shape the lid. Position and glue on top of the narrow end of the eyelet with the trimmed disc resting against the side of the eyelet to create the effect of a hinge.

# MAKING THE PEN WIPE

Take the bundle of bristles and poke through the eyelet from the widest end. Neaten and flatten the bristles at the widest end of the eyelet and rub over with tacky glue. Once they are glued, neatly trim the bristles to protrude out of the narrow end of the eyelet by ¹⁄₁₆in (1.5mm) using sharp scissors.

# MAKING THE PEN

Take the wire and use the flat section in a pair of pliers to flatten one end, approximately ⅛in (3mm). Shape the flattened wire into a nib shape using either small sharp scissors or needle files. Trim the pen to measure ⁹⁄₁₆in (14mm) long and sand the straight end smooth if necessary. Paint the handle of the pen and the end of the nib with black enamel paint.

# MAKING THE PENCIL

Stain the length of centre cane. Once dry, use a sharp craft knife to carefully shave the tip at one end to a point. Mix a small amount of black and silver acrylic paint and dip the point of the pencil into the mixture to make the lead. Trim the pencil to measure ½in (13mm) long and touch up the straight end of the pencil with wood stain.

# MAKING THE ROCKER BLOTTER

Cut the dowel piece in half to make the rocker and lightly sand. Take the double column and cut off one end to make a tiny knob. Retain the remainder of the double column for the paperclip. Lightly stain the rocker and knob. Glue the grey blotting paper on to the curved edge of the wood and position and glue the knob centrally on to the straight edge of the rocker.

# MAKING THE PAPERCLIP

Take the base wood piece and gently round off the corners. Take the double column and cut off one of the disc sections. Lightly stain the base and disc with wood stain. Glue the disc centrally on to one end of the base. Position and glue the eye of the metal filigree to rest on the tiny disc as shown.

# MAKING THE SEAL & SEALING WAX

Trim most of the straight end off the belaying pin handle leaving approximately ¹⁄₁₆in (1.5mm) attached and lightly stain with wood stain. Glue the inset side of the tiny metal cap on to the protruding straight end of the belaying pin handle to make the seal. Cut a stick of polymer clay ¼ x ¹⁄₁₆in (6 x 1.5mm) to make the stick of sealing wax. Follow the manufacturer's instructions to bake in a domestic oven.

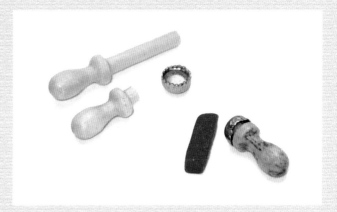

# MAKING THE LETTER OPENER

Take the brad and open out a clip and remove. Position and glue the straight end of the clip on top of one of the handle wood pieces with the shaped end protruding by ⁵⁄₁₆in (8mm). Position the other handle piece on top. Once dry, hold the end of the wood and form the part nearest to the blade into a handle shape using a needle file. Trim the end of the wood so that the whole knife measures no more than ⁵⁄₈in (16mm) long. Sand the cut end smooth and colour the handle using wood stain.

# MAKING THE MAGNIFYING GLASS

Trim the straight end off the belaying pin to make the handle and sand smooth. Paint the handle with black enamel paint. Once dry, glue the jump ring on to the flat end of the handle and once secure, fill the ring with 3D gloss varnish to create the effect of a lens.

# ❧ Gramophone ❧

I N AMERICA IN **1877**, THOMAS EDISON INVENTED THE PHONOGRAPH, A MACHINE THAT PRODUCED MUSIC FROM RECORDINGS IN METAL CYLINDERS. A DECADE LATER AN IMPROVED DEVICE, CALLED THE GRAMOPHONE, WAS CREATED THAT COULD PLAY FLAT DISCS. CONTINUAL IMPROVEMENTS IN THE MECHANISM, SOUND QUALITY AND NUMBERS OF RECORDINGS WHICH COULD BE PLAYED ON THE GRAMOPHONE WERE MADE DURING THE EDWARDIAN ERA INCREASING ITS POPULARITY.

**Dimensions** 1⅞in (48mm) high; 1½in (38mm) wide; 1⅝in (41mm) deep
**Skill level** Advanced
**Templates** Page 160

## MATERIALS & EQUIPMENT

♠ **From ⅛in (3mm) thick obechi wood:**
− 1¼ x 1¼in (32 x 32mm) for base

♠ **From 1⁄16in (1.5mm) thick obechi wood:**
− Two ⅞ x 5⁄16in (22 x 8mm) for sides
− 1³⁄16 x 1³⁄16in (30 x 30mm) for top
− Two 1⅛ x 1⅛in (29 x 29mm) for dividers
− Two 1 x 5⁄16in (25 x 8mm) front and back

♠ **From 1⁄16in (1.5mm) diameter round brass tube:**
− 1¹⁄16in (27mm) length for arm

♠ **From 3⁄32in (2.5mm) diameter round brass tube:**
− ⅜in (10mm) length for shoulder

♠ **From 26-gauge (0.45mm) gold-plated wire:**
− 9⁄16in (14mm) length for crank
− 1⁵⁄16in (33mm) for wire support

♠ **From pewter embossing sheet:**
− 1in (25mm) diameter round disc for turntable

♠ **From brass embossing sheet:**
− 1⁄16in (1.5mm) diameter round disc for sound box cover
− ¾ x 1⁄16in (19 x 1.5mm) for fastener

♠ Brass sequin pin for centre spindle

♠ 1in (25mm) diameter round disc of adhesive green felt for turntable felt

♠ 9⁄16in (14mm) wooden belaying pin for crank handle

- ♠ 1mm gold-plated crimp bead for crank cap
- ♠ Miniature plastic French horn for horn
- ♠ Large brass hollow rivet contact (electrical eyelet) for sound box
- ♠ ⅛in (3mm) brass eyelet for horn connector
- ♠ Gold-plated earring clip for arm holder

- ♠ Wood stain
- ♠ Beeswax polish
- ♠ Brown or brass-coloured spray paint
- ♠ Super glue gel
- ♠ Tacky glue

# MAKING THE GRAMOPHONE

**1** Take one of the side wood pieces and transfer the hole position from the side template. Use a ¹⁄₃₂in (1mm) drill bit to drill the hole.

**2** Take the top wood piece and one divider wood piece and use a ¹⁄₃₂in (1mm) drill bit to drill a hole through the centre of each.

**3** Take the top wood piece and round all edges on both sides of the wood using fine-grade sandpaper. Repeat the procedure with the two divider wood pieces and round the edges on one side only of the base wood piece. Lightly sand and sparingly stain the wood pieces to avoid them warping.
**TIP** Ensure the drill holes remain visible after staining and polishing.

**4** Place the top and the divider wood piece with the drilled hole together. The grain of each wood piece should run in the same direction and the drill holes in each should match up. Secure the pieces together with tacky glue.

**5** Position the base wood piece with the rounded edges facing upwards. Position and glue the remaining divider wood piece centrally on top with the grain in each running in the same direction. Polish the two constructions together with all the remaining wood pieces with beeswax polish.

**6** Place the side wood pieces between the front and back wood pieces. All pieces rest on their narrow edges and all outside edges are flush. The side piece with the drilled hole should be positioned on the right hand side of the construction with the hole positioned at the top back. ☞

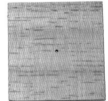

7 Position centrally on top of the base construction with the grain of wood in the front and back pieces running in line with the grain of the wood in the base piece and the drilled hole in the side positioned as before.

8 Take the centre spindle pin and insert up into the divider piece in the top construction, so that the point of the pin protrudes over the top piece by ³⁄₃₂in (2.5mm). Trim the excess pin on the underside and apply a little super glue gel to hold. **TIP** It doesn't need to be trimmed flat as the end will be hidden inside the gramophone.

9 Position and glue the turntable felt on top of the turntable and drill a ¹⁄₃₂in (1mm) hole centrally through each. Locate the hole on top of the central spindle and glue into place. Glue the top section on to the main construction with the grain of the wood running in line with the base piece.

10 To make the crank handle cut the straight end off the belaying pin. Drill a hole into the flat end of the belaying pin, using a ¹⁄₃₂in (1mm) drill bit and then stain and polish. Take the piece of crank wire and shape on top of the gramophone's crank template. Glue the shorter end into the drilled hole in the belaying pin as shown.

11 Thread the crank cap on to the crank into the position shown. Thread the end of the crank into the drilled hole in the side of the gramophone. Glue the bead and crank into place using a dab of super glue gel.

12 Take the horn and carefully shave off the piping with a sharp craft knife and sand smooth. Cut the bell to measure 1in (25mm) long and spray all over with paint inside and out. **TIP** Drill a ¹⁄₃₂in (1mm) hole into the end of the bell and insert the end of a cocktail stick. Place the opposite end of the cocktail stick in a temporary holder whilst spray painting to allow an even coverage.

13 Insert the wire support inside the brass tube arm piece, allowing an equal overlap at each end. Position the narrow end of the sound box rivet contact on to one end of the wire, and slide and glue the shoulder brass tube piece on to the arm at the opposite end. Glue into place with super glue gel. The ends of the tube pieces are flush.

14 Position the narrow end of the horn connector eyelet on to the end of the shoulder with the wide end flush with the end of the tube. Hold the arm carefully with pliers and bend into the angled position as shown.

15 Hold the arm below the shoulder and bend the arm into the shape as shown.

16 Thread the wire protruding from the horn connector into the hole drilled in the end of the horn using a dab of super glue gel. Use pliers to bend the arm below the sound box to the side as shown. Position and glue the brass sound box cover disc on to the end of the sound box.

17 Take the arm holder and remove the disc from the back of the clip using small pliers. Trim the two side pieces off each side of the clip as shown. Position and glue the end of the post on to the back of the arm using super glue gel as shown.

18 Take the fastener brass strip piece and wind and glue around the arm and arm holder to further secure the hold. Position the bottom of the arm holder on to the back of the gramophone and super glue into place.

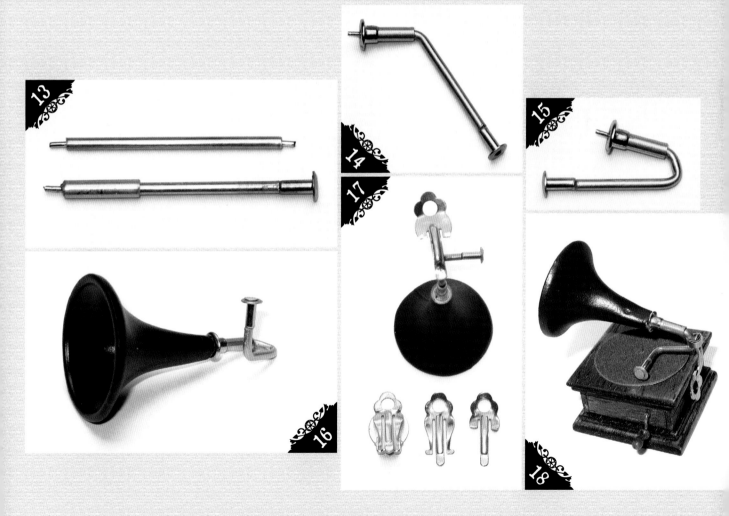

# ❊ Arts & Crafts Gramophone Table ❊

**M**USIC WAS A POPULAR SOCIAL AND FAMILY ENTERTAINMENT DURING THE EDWARDIAN ERA. MIDDLE-CLASS HOME-OWNERS WERE THRILLED WITH BEING ABLE TO POSSESS A GRAMOPHONE AND BRING THE BEST OF THE THEATRE STAGE INTO THEIR HOMES. DESPITE THIS THE EDWARDIANS THOUGHT THE DESIGN OF THE GRAMOPHONES CUMBERSOME AND A SIMPLY DESIGNED ARTS & CRAFTS-STYLE TABLE POSITIONED IN THE CORNER OF THE LIVING ROOM MADE AN IDEAL STAND FOR THE RECORD PLAYER.

**Dimensions**  2⅝in (67mm) high; 1⅝in (41mm) wide; 1⅝in (41mm) deep
**Skill level**  Beginner
**Templates**  Page 160

# MATERIALS & EQUIPMENT

♠ **From ⅛in (3mm) thick obechi sheet wood:**
– Four 1 x ⅝in (25 x 16mm) for top supports
– 1¼ x 1¼in (31 x 31mm) for shelf
– Four 1 x ⅛in (25 x 3mm) for shelf supports
– 1⅝ x 1⅝in (41 x 41mm) for top

♠ **From ³⁄₁₆ x ³⁄₁₆in (3 x 3mm) obechi strip wood:**
– Four 2½in (64mm) lengths for legs

♠ **From ¾in (19mm) hardwood dowel:**
– 3in (76mm) length for sanding tool

♠ Oak wood stain

♠ Tacky glue

♠ Beeswax polish

# MAKING THE ARTS & CRAFTS GRAMAPHONE TABLE

**1** Take the top support wood pieces and measure and mark half way along one long edge on each using a pencil. Wind and glue a piece of fine-grade sandpaper around the piece of dowel to make a sanding tool.

**2** Position the sanding tool on top of the pencil marks and sand approximately ³⁄₁₆in (5mm) down into the wood pieces as shown. **OPTIONAL** Pierce a heart decoration following steps 7 and 8 on page 16.

**3** Transfer the shelf template on to the shelf wood piece and cut out. To prevent the wood splitting, first cut against the grain, using either mitre cutters or a craft knife, and then cut with the grain of the wood. Lightly sand and stain each of the wooden pieces.

**4** Position and glue a top support piece between two legs. The top of the support piece should be flush with the tops of the legs. Leave a gap of ¼in (6mm) at the bottom of the legs and position and glue a shelf support into place. Repeat the procedure with the remaining legs, a top support and a shelf support. **TIP** Use a right-angled gluing jig at each stage to ensure the construction dries square.

**5** Take the shelf wood piece and position and glue the two remaining shelf support pieces on top of the shelf wood piece, with the grain running in line. All outside edges should be flush.

**6** Place a leg construction with the inset side facing downwards. Glue the shelf to rest on the shelf support as shown. Glue a top support piece on to each leg in line with the previously positioned top supports. The insides of the top supports should be flush with the inside edges of the legs.

**7** Glue the remaining leg construction into place with the inset side facing outwards. Position and glue the top centrally on top of the table ensuring that the grain runs in line with the shelf wood piece. Once dry, polish the table with beeswax polish.

# Wall Shelves

SMALL SETS OF HANGING WALL SHELVES USED TO DISPLAY BOOKS AND DECORATIVE WARES BECAME PARTICULARLY POPULAR DURING THE NINETEENTH CENTURY. EDWARDIAN WALL SHELVES WERE OFTEN MUCH LIGHTER AND LESS ORNATE THEN THEIR PREDECESSORS AND WERE OFTEN PAINTED IN WHITE OR CREAM. WALL SHELVES MADE OUT OF OAK AND MAHOGANY WERE ALSO FASHIONABLE. DESIGNS DIFFERED; SOME HAD TIERED SHELVING, WHILE OTHERS WERE OPEN AT THE BACK. SHELVING THAT WAS CLOSED AT THE BACK ALLOWED FOR A MORE SOLID CONSTRUCTION.

**Dimensions** 2½in (64mm) high; 2⅞in (73mm) wide; ½in (13mm) deep

**Skill level** Beginner

**Template** Page 160

## MATERIALS & EQUIPMENT

♠ **From ¹⁄₁₆in (1.5mm) thick obechi wood:**

– 2¾ x ½in (70 x 13mm) for top board

– 2¾ x ¾in (70 x 19mm) for bottom board (grain to run with the short length)

– Three 2¾ x ½in (70 x 13mm) for bottom shelves

– Two 2¼ x ½in (57 x 13mm) for sides

– 2¾ x ⁷⁄₁₆in (70 x 11mm) for top shelf

– Two ³⁄₈ x ¹⁄₁₆in (10 x 1.5mm) for shelf supports

♠ Acrylic paint

♠ Tacky glue

## Why not try...

...making the wall shelves out of mahogany wood and finishing them with beeswax polish.

# MAKING THE WALL SHELVES

1 Transfer the top board template on to the top board wood piece and cut out.

2 Take the bottom board and measure and mark every ¼in (6mm) along the length of the wood. Use a scoring tool to score along the marked lines to create the effect of panels. Lightly sand the wooden components and paint them sparingly to avoid the pieces warping. Once dry, very lightly sand the surfaces on all sides to smooth the finish of the paint. If necessary, re-paint and repeat the procedure. Buff the pieces to produce a dull sheen using a piece of kitchen paper towel.

3 Position a bottom shelf on to each of the bottom board's long edges. All outside edges are flush. Place the construction between the two side pieces; the ends of the sides should be flush with the bottom shelf. **TIP** Use a right-angled gluing jig at all stages to ensure that the construction dries square.

4 Slot and glue the top board inside the top of the construction, so that the angled section only is protruding at the sides. Glue the top shelf to rest on the top board; the top edges of the side pieces should slightly protrude from the top shelf.

5 Glue the two shelf supports on top of the remaining bottom shelf, one at each end. One end of the shelf supports should be flush with the back of the shelf.

6 Position and glue the remaining shelf centrally into the opening with the shelf supports facing downwards and the ends flush with the back of the construction.

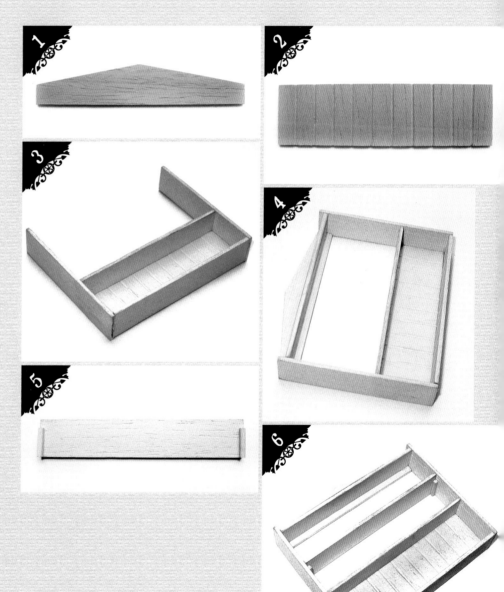

# ⊰⊹ Tiffany Table Lamp ⊹⊱

American Art Nouveau exponent Louis Comfort Tiffany designed and produced decorative glassware for the home at the turn of the twentieth century. Lamps with bronze bases were frequently shaped to imitate naturalistic forms such as stems, and trunks supported colourful floral leaded glass shades with an integrated theme such as trees in blossom. Tiffany lamps became highly desired and 'Tiffany style' designs were imitated around the world.

**Dimensions** 1⁷⁄₁₆in (37mm) high; 1in (25mm) wide
**Skill level** Beginner

## Materials & Equipment

- ♠ ⅝ x ¼in (16 x 6mm) tapered serrated gold-plated bead for column
- ♠ ⅜in (10mm) gold-plated bead cap for base
- ♠ ³⁄₁₆in (5mm) diameter round serrated gold-plated bead for neck
- ♠ 1in x ½in (25mm x 13mm) for gold-plated filigree shade for lamp shade
- ♠ ⅛ x ¹⁄₁₆in (3 x 1.5mm) for gold-plated disc for finial
- ♠ ⅞in (22mm) gold-plated spoke for shade holder
- ♠ 12-volt grain of rice bulb with fine wire for bulb
- ♠ Metallic old gold or bronze spray paint
- ♠ Glass paint
- ♠ Super glue gel

## Why not try...

...replacing the spoke with an upturned ⁵⁄₁₆in (8mm) diameter serrated gold plated bead cap and the shade with an ¹¹⁄₁₆ x ½in (17 x 13mm) Lucite bell flower to create a differently styled Art Nouveau lamp. Instead of spray painting the stand, create a patina by lightly covering the metal with a dark brown, spirit-based wood stain.

# MAKING THE TIFFANY TABLE LAMP

**1** Position and glue the wide end of the column bead centrally on top of the domed base using super glue gel. Take the neck bead and position and glue on top of the column with all openings running in line.

**2** Take the shade and the disc finial. Position and glue the flat side of the finial centrally on top of the shade.

**3** Take the shade holder and use a pair of small pliers to slightly lift the loops at each end. Check the shaped shade holder fits inside the shade and the ends of the loops sit neatly and equally against the inside of the shade.

**4** Position the centre of the shade holder on top of the neck in the position shown and glue into place. Spray paint the stand and the inside and outside of the shade with old gold- or bronze-coloured spray paint.

**5** Take the shade and, beginning at the top, start to fill the gaps with glass paint using a small fine paintbrush. Work symmetrically around the shade and allow each colour to dry before continuing with the next.

**6** Thread the bulb wires down through the stand and rest the end of the bulb on the neck. Position the shade to rest on top of the shade holder. Do not glue the shade on top of the spokes to allow the easy replacement of the bulb.

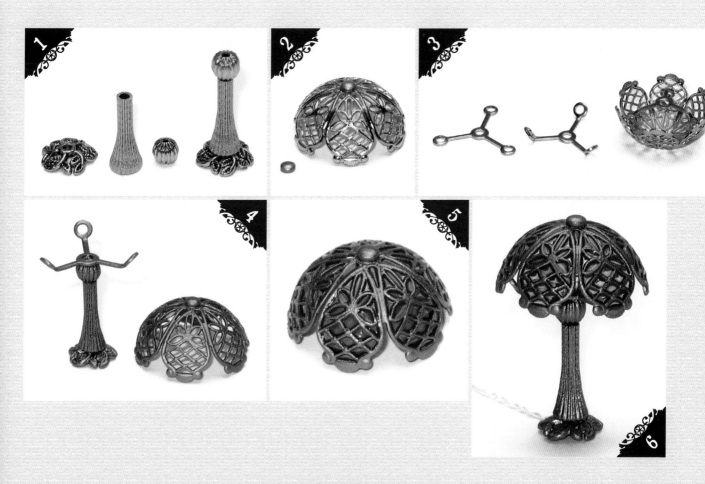

# Brownie Box Camera

Amateur photography was revolutionalised in 1900 by the Eastman Kodak Company in New York when they mass-produced a very affordable brownie box roll-film camera. The camera was simple to use and was basically a cardboard box, covered in black leatherette with a lens in one end and film in the other. Amateur photography was a new national pastime and sales of brownie box cameras boomed.

**Dimensions** $\frac{7}{16}$in (11mm) high; $\frac{3}{8}$in (10mm) wide; $\frac{1}{2}$in (13mm) deep
**Skill level** Intermediate

## Materials & Equipment

♠ **From ¼in (6mm) thick obechi wood:**
~ ½ x ⅜in (13 x 10mm) for box

♠ **From ¹⁄₁₆in (1.5mm) thick obechi wood:**
~ ½ x ⅜in (13 x 10mm) for box

♠ **From fine black leatherette paper:**
~ Two ½ x ½in (13 x 13mm) for end casings
~ 1½ x ⅝in (38 x 16mm) for outside casing
~ ½ x ⁵⁄₁₆in (13 x 5mm) for strap

♠ **From ¹⁄₁₆in (1.5mm) diameter round brass tube:**
~ Two ¹⁄₆₄in (0.5mm) thick pieces for front viewfinder covers

♠ **From ¹⁄₁₆in (1.5mm) wide square brass tube:**
~ Two ¹⁄₆₄in (0.5mm) thick pieces for top and side viewfinder covers

♠ **From ¹⁄₁₆in (1.5mm) diameter round aluminium tube:**
~ ¹⁄₆₄in (0.5mm) thick piece for film advance cover

♠ Small brass hollow rivet contact (electrical eyelet) for lens holder

♠ Two ⅛in (3mm) long brass pins for strap pins

♠ Cocktail stick for handle former

♠ ¹⁄₃₂in (1mm) wide cotter pin for film advance lever

♠ Black enamel paint

♠ Super glue gel

♠ Tacky glue

# MAKING THE BROWNIE BOX CAMERA

**1** Take the two box wood pieces and glue wide side together with tacky glue to form a block. Lightly sand all surfaces smooth. Cover the two ends of the wooden block with a thin even layer of tacky glue and attach the end casing paper pieces. Once dry, trim the paper to the same size as the block ends with sharp scissors.

**2** Cover the outside of the wooden block with a thin, even layer of tacky glue. Take the outside casing paper piece and fold and secure around the block, beginning and ending on a narrow side for the bottom of the camera. **TIP** Allow the paper to overlap the block on each side and once dry, trim excess paper to the same size as the block.

**3** Use a pin vice with a 1/16in (1.5mm) drill bit to drill a hole centrally and partway down into one end of the covered wooden block. Paint the wide end of the lens holder with black enamel paint and once dry, insert and glue the narrow end into the drilled hole.

**4** Take the strap paper piece and fold and glue in half width ways. Once dry, cut a strip to measure 7/16in (11mm) by 1/16in (1.5mm). Place the centre over a cocktail stick to shape and position and glue on top of the camera cover as shown. Insert the strap pins through each end of the strap and into the wooden block.

**5** Paint one side of the brass view finder covers with black enamel paint. Once dry, position and glue on to the camera as shown using a dab of super glue gel. Take the film advance cover and glue on to the side of the camera as shown.
**TIP** Thread the viewfinder cover pieces on to the end of a cocktail stick to sand, smooth and paint.

**6** Take the cotter pin and cut in half. Take one piece and partially fold over 1/16in (1.5mm) at one end with pliers. Cut a 1/4in (6mm) length off the other piece and position and super glue in to the folded end, pressing the fold with pliers to further secure. Once dry, cut the cross piece to measure 3/32in (2.5mm) long by trimming each end equally. Trim the upright piece to measure 3/16in (5mm) long and carefully hold and press the end into the centre of the film advance cover and into the side of the wooden block.

Kitchen Dresser
- page 94

Kitchen Table - page 86

# THE KITCHEN

# IN THE KITCHEN

**T**HE KITCHEN WAS GENERALLY situated at the back of newly built Edwardian middle-class homes and was a room that visitors would not have been permitted to enter. The kitchen was often smaller than its Victorian predecessor due to a desire for improved and more hygienic working conditions. Its use was purely functional for the preparation of food. A separate scullery room attached to the kitchen would have been used for the laundry.

For the growing numbers of middle-class households, employing domestic staff was a good way of signifying their status. Usually a maid would have been employed to clean and undertake the menial chores and a cook to prepare the family's meals. As it became more difficult to find domestic help due to the increase in middle-class households outnumbering available staff, it did become more common for the lady of the house to accept the role of cooking.

The main feature of the kitchen was a coal-fired range, used for cooking meals, providing hot water and heating the room. Absorbent rugs were often placed in front to prevent the floor from becoming slippery from spillage. Stoneware or porcelain rectangular or square sinks, with sloping draining boards, which had previously only been found in the scullery were now located in the kitchen, often with a wooden plate rack above for draining.

Pine dressers with open shelves for storing crockery and a cupboard for storing other kitchen accessories were popular and were often built in. Larders with cool, tiled shelves and mesh-covered doors stored and preserved fresh food whilst a pantry or cupboard stored other food away from the heat from the range. Cooking utensils and labour-saving devices were plentiful during the Edwardian era and sales of cookery books flourished.

In the centre of the kitchen a pine table would have been used for the preparation of food, and the tabletop would have been scrubbed daily with a mixture of sand and soda. A piece of marble may have stood on top for pastry-making. A hanging lamp was generally situated above the table.

As hygiene was an important aspect, kitchen walls would have been painted either in washable distemper or covered with wallpaper and varnished. Light, bright colours were popular, such as green and cream and the ceiling would have been whitewashed annually. Woodwork was generally painted in white or sometimes in dark green or brown. Books and magazines on home styling suggested that the areas around sinks and the range should be covered with white tiles for cleanliness.

Red quarry tiles were popular on the kitchen floor, as were wooden floorboards, often covered with washable patterned linoleum.

# ❧ Kitchen Table ❧

A CENTRAL STURDY WORKTABLE WAS AN ESSENTIAL PIECE OF FURNITURE IN ANY EDWARDIAN KITCHEN AND WAS USED FOR THE PREPARATION OF FOOD. FURNITURE DESIGN WAS NOT CONSIDERED AS IMPORTANT IN THE KITCHEN AS IN OTHER ROOMS, AND IN MANY HOMES PIECES FROM THE PREVIOUS ERA WOULD STILL HAVE BEEN IN USE. AS HYGIENE WAS THE MOST IMPORTANT CONSIDERATION, THE TABLE TOP WOULD HAVE BEEN SCRUBBED DAILY.

**Dimensions** 2$^{15}$⁄$_{32}$in (63mm) high; 3¾in (95mm) wide; 2⅛in (54mm) deep

**Skill level** Beginner

**Templates** Page 161

# MATERIALS & EQUIPMENT

♠ **From ³⁄₃₂in (2.5mm) obechi sheet wood:**

– 3¾ x 2⅛in (95 x 54mm) for table top

– 1$^{15}$⁄$_{32}$ x $^{11}$⁄$_{32}$in (37 x 9mm) for drawer front

♠ **From ¹⁄₁₆in (1.5mm) obechi sheet wood:**

– 3½ by 1⅞in (89 x 48mm) for drawer support

– 1$^{15}$⁄$_{32}$ x $^{11}$⁄$_{32}$in (37 x 9mm) for drawer back

– Two 1¹⁄₁₆ x $^{11}$⁄$_{32}$in (27 x 9mm) for drawer sides

– 1$^{11}$⁄$_{32}$ x 1¹⁄₁₆in (34 x 27mm) for drawer base

– Two 1¹⁄₁₆ x ¼in (27 x 6mm) for drawer dividers

♠ **From ⅜ x ⅛in (10 x 3mm) obechi strip wood:**

– Two 3⅛in (79mm) lengths for long supports

– 1½in (38mm) length for short support

♠ **From ³⁄₁₆ x ³⁄₁₆in (5 x 5mm) obechi strip wood:**

– 1½in (38mm) length for drawer stop

♠ Four ³⁄₁₆in (5mm) square wooden spindles for legs

♠ Two ³⁄₃₂in (2.5mm) diameter wooden drawer knobs

♠ Oak or pine wood stain

♠ Light grey and white acrylic paint

♠ Tacky glue

# MAKING THE KITCHEN TABLE

**1** Take a wooden spindle leg and measure and mark 2⅜in (60mm) from the turned end. Remove the waste from the square end of the spindle leg using a mitre block and saw. Repeat the procedure with the remaining spindle legs.

**2** Take the table top wood piece and measure and mark every ¹¹⁄₃₂in (9mm) along the width of the wood. Use a scoring tool to score along the marked lines to create the effect of panels. **NOTE** Imperial measurements will make the last panel slightly wider.

**3** Transfer the drawer support template on to the drawer support wood piece and cut out. To avoid the wood splitting, first cut against the grain of the wood using either mitre cutters or a craft knife and then with the grain of the wood.

**4** Transfer the drill hole positions from the drawer front template on to the drawer front. Use a pin vice with a ¹⁄₁₆in (1.5mm) drill bit to drill holes through the wood. Lightly sand all of the wood pieces and stain sparingly to prevent the wood warping.

**5** Glue the drawer knobs into the holes in the drawer front wood piece. Glue the drawer front, back and side wood pieces on to the outside edges of the drawer base wood piece.

**6** Take the drawer divider wood pieces and position and glue inside the drawer, allowing equal gaps between each for cutlery. ☞

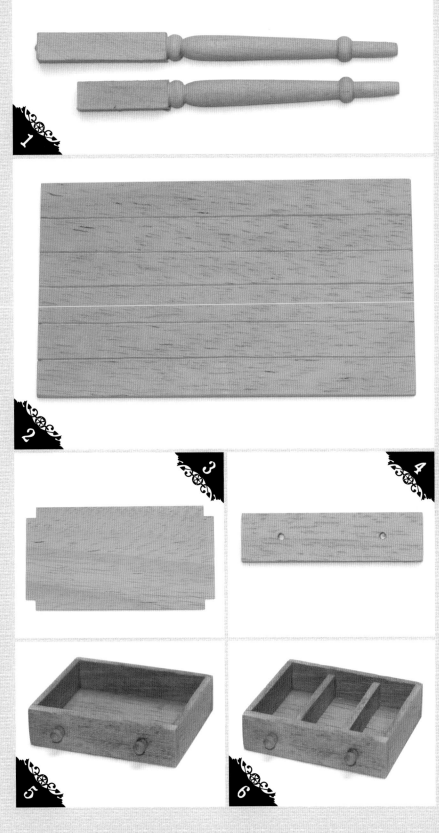

**7** Take the drawer support wood piece. Position and glue the narrow edges of the long and the short support wood pieces on top as shown with all outside edges flush.

**8** Place the drawer into the open end of the construction, with the drawer front flush with the edge of the drawer support. Position and glue the drawer stop wood piece immediately behind the drawer. Remove the drawer and allow the glue to dry.

**9** Position and glue the construction centrally on to the underside of table top as shown and position and glue the straight ends of the legs to rest in the cut out sections. Ensure that they stand straight before leaving them to dry.

**10** Slide the drawer into position. To add the effect of a scrubbed table top, dry brush (page 179) the table top with white and light grey acrylic paint.

# ✥ Sink and Draining Board ✥

**B**Y THE TURN OF THE TWENTIETH CENTURY VAST IMPROVEMENTS HAD BEEN MADE IN PUBLIC WATER SUPPLY AND HOT WATER SYSTEMS, RESULTING IN MANY KITCHEN SINKS BEING SUPPLIED WITH HOT AND COLD RUNNING WATER. PORCELAIN SINKS, EITHER SHALLOW OR DEEP, THAT STOOD ON BRICK PILLARS WITH GROOVED, SLOPING, WOODEN DRAINING BOARDS WERE IN CONSTANT USE FOR THE PREPARATION OF FOOD AND THE WASHING OF DISHES.

**Dimensions** 3¼in (82mm) high; 4⁵⁄₁₆in (106mm) wide; 1½in (38mm) deep
**Skill level** Advanced
**Templates** Page 161

# MATERIALS & EQUIPMENT

♠ **From ¼in (6mm) thick obechi sheet wood:**
– Two 2¼ x 1½in (57 x 38mm) for sink pillars
– 3 x 1½in (76 x 38mm) for drainer pillar

♠ **From ⅛in (3mm) thick obechi sheet wood:**
– 1¾ x 1¼in (44 x 32mm) for sink base
– Two 2 x ⅝in (50 x 16mm) for sink sides
– Two 1¼ x ⅝in (32 x 16mm) for sink ends

♠ **From 1⁄16in (1.5mm) thick obechi sheet wood:**
– ¹⁵⁄₃₂ x ⁵⁄₁₆in (12 x 8mm) for overflow front
– Two ¹⁵⁄₃₂ x ¹⁄₁₆in (12 x 1.5mm) for overflow sides
– 2¼ x 1⅜in (57 x 35mm) for draining board base
– Two 2⁵⁄₁₆ x ¼in (58.5 x 6mm) for draining board sides
– 1⅜ x ¼in (35 x 6mm) for draining board end

♠ **From 220 grit (grade 0) sandpaper:**
– 5 x 5in (127 x 127mm) piece for bricks

♠ **From ⅛in (3mm) diameter aluminium tube:**
– 2½in (64mm) length for waste pipe

♠ Two ⅛in (3mm) nickel eyelets for waste pipe support and plug surround

♠ Tube bender

♠ Brick- and mortar-coloured acrylic paint for bricks

♠ White and light grey acrylic paint for dry brushing

♠ Oak or pine wood stain

♠ Sanding sealer

♠ White enamel paint

♠ Varnish

♠ Tacky glue

♠ Super glue gel

# MAKING THE SINK AND DRAINING BOARD

**1** Paint the abrasive side of the sandpaper in sections with different brick-coloured acrylic paints. Once dry, cut out bricks to measure ¾ x ¼in (19 x 6mm) and mix up. **TIP** Slightly watering down the acrylic paint creates a softer and more natural finish to the bricks.

**2** Take the sink and drainer pillars and paint with a mortar-coloured grey acrylic paint. Once dry, take a sink pillar and position the bricks on to one side following a standard stretcher bond pattern and secure into place using tacky glue. Glue any overlapping brick on to the edge of the pillar and once dry, trim to size. **TIP** The opposite edge of the pillar will be positioned against the wall so will not require bricking.

**3** Continue the brick pattern up the pillar to the top and trim any excess brick using small, sharp scissors. Fill in the gaps on the edge of the pillar with any brick off-cuts and then turn over and repeat the mirror image procedure on the other side. Repeat the bricking process with the remaining pillars and bricks.

**4** Take the sink base and transfer the drill hole measurement from the sink base template. Firstly drill a ¹⁄₁₆in (1.5mm) drill hole and then open out the hole using either a needle file or a ⁵⁄₃₂in (4mm) drill bit.

**5** Position and glue the sink ends and sink sides on to the outside edge of the sink base piece. Sand the edges round at the top of the

sink using fine-grade sandpaper and then sand the ends in a circular motion to smooth. **TIP** Use a right-angled gluing jig at each stage to ensure that the construction dries square.

**6** Take the overflow front piece and chamfer one short edge and two long edges on one side only of the wood piece. Take the overflow side pieces and position on top of the flat side of the overflow front piece as shown. All outside edges are flush. Once dry, sand and smooth all outside edges.

**7** Position and glue the overflow section against the inside of the sink as shown. Seal the sink with a coat of sanding sealer. Once

the sink is dry, paint with white enamel paint. Apply a coat of varnish to create the effect of porcelain.

8 Transfer the draining board base template on to the draining board base wood piece. Make grooves in the wood ¹⁄₁₆in (1.5mm) wide and ¹⁄₃₂in (1mm) deep, by firstly scoring along the marked lines and then using a needle file to make a channel in between the scored lines.

9 Take the draining board side pieces and round one corner on each. Lightly stain all the draining board pieces and once dry, position the sides and end on to the outside edges of the draining board base piece as shown. **TIP** To add the effect of water damage to the wood, dry brush (page 179) the draining board with white and light grey acrylic paint.

10 Make a simple waste pipe by placing the aluminium tube in a tube bender and bend to slightly curve the centre. Use a junior hacksaw and mitre block to trim the straight end of the tube to measure ⁷⁄₈in (22mm) long and the curve to protrude by ¹⁄₈in (3mm). Sand the long end of the waste pipe to an angle as shown to fit against a wall at a later stage.

11 Position and glue a sink pillar on to the underside of the sink with the full bricks positioned against the base of the sink as shown and all outside edges flush. Slide the narrow end of the waste pipe support eyelet on to the short end of the tube until both ends are flush. Position and glue, using super glue gel, immediately below the plug hole opening and position the opposite end of the tubing to rest flat against the work surface.

12 Position and glue the narrow end of the plug surround into the hole in the sink. Dry fit the remaining pillars and drainer support as shown. Ensure full bricks are positioned at the top of the pillars. The top of the drainer pillar should be gently chamfered (page 178) to match the slope of the drainer before gluing the pieces into position.

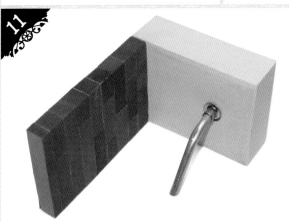

# ❧ Plate Rack ❧

Wall-mounted, wooden plate racks originated in the late eighteenth century. During the Edwardian era plate racks were practically situated on the wall close to the sink to dry and safely store the crockery. As equipment for other chores was often placed around the sink area, they also avoided the draining board becoming too cluttered.

**Dimensions** 1⁷⁄₁₆in (37mm) high; 1¹⁵⁄₁₆in (49mm) wide; ⅝in (16mm) deep
**Skill level** Intermediate

## MATERIALS & EQUIPMENT

♠ **From ⅛in (3mm) thick bass sheet wood:**
- Four 1¹¹⁄₁₆ x ³⁄₁₆in (43 x 5mm) for supports
- Two 1⁷⁄₁₆ x ⅝in (37 x 16mm) for sides

♠ **From ¹⁄₁₆in (1.5mm) thick bass sheet wood:**
- 1¹¹⁄₁₆ x 1¹⁄₁₆in (43 x 27mm) for back

♠ **From ³⁄₆₄in (1mm) thick hardwood dowel:**
- Eight 1¼in (32mm) lengths for slats

♠ Masking tape

♠ Pine or oak wood stain

♠ White and pale grey acrylic paint

♠ Tacky glue

## Why not try...

...spraying aluminium dinner plates with white or cream spray paint and decorating with floral designs popular during the Edwardian era, by either painting or applying water slide decals. Cover the plates with 3D gloss varnish to create a porcelain effect.

# MAKING THE PLATE RACK

**1** Take one of the support wood pieces and position it to rest on its narrow edge. Measure and mark every ³⁄₁₆in (4.8mm) centrally along the facing narrow edge. Repeat the procedure with another of the support wood pieces.

**2** Use a pin vice with a ³⁄₆₄in (1mm) drill bit to drill half way down into the wood pieces at each marked position. To determine the correct drilling depth wind a thin strip of masking tape ³⁄₃₂in (2.5mm) from the end of the drill bit. Lightly sand each of the wood pieces and then sparingly stain.

**3** Take one of the drilled supports and starting from one end carefully insert and glue a slat into position. Repeat the procedure until all the slats have been inserted. **TIP** If the slats are a very tight fit it may help to make the holes larger using a slightly wider drill bit to avoid the delicate dowel from breaking.

**4** Take the other drilled support and carefully slot and glue the ends of the slats into each of the drilled holes.

**5** Take the two remaining support wood pieces and place wide side down with the back wood piece positioned and glued in between as shown. The back piece is inset between the two support pieces.

**6** Place the side pieces to rest on their long narrow edges and position and glue the back construction in-between with the inset side facing forwards. All outside edges are flush.

**7** Stand the construction and position and glue the slatted front section inside the opening. All outside edges are flush. To create the effect of water damage on to the wood, dry brush (page 179) the plate rack with white and pale grey acrylic paint.

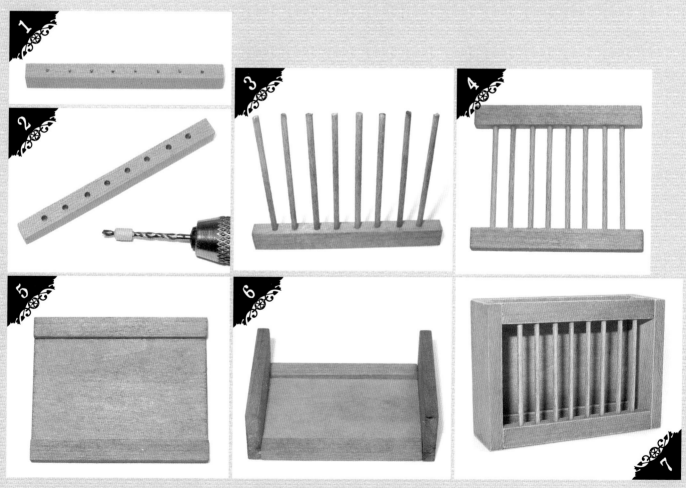

# Kitchen Dresser

THE DRESSER EVOLVED FROM A SIDE TABLE PLACED AGAINST A WALL BELOW A SET OF OPEN SHELVES. DURING THE LATE SEVENTEENTH CENTURY, THE TWO WERE COMBINED AND THE ADDITION OF A SHELF BACKBOARD TOGETHER WITH DRAWERS AND CUPBOARDS OR POT BOARDS FOR STORAGE MADE THE DRESSER INTO AN INDISPENSIBLE PIECE OF KITCHEN FURNITURE FOR THE EDWARDIANS. DESIGNS OF DRESSERS WERE GENERALLY REGIONAL.

**Dimensions** $6^{17}/_{32}$in (166.5mm) high; $4^{1}/_{8}$in (105mm) wide; $1^{1}/_{2}$in (38mm) deep
**Skill level** Advanced
**Templates** Pages 162

# MATERIALS & EQUIPMENT

♠ **From ⅛in (3mm) thick obechi sheet wood:**

- Four $1^{13}/_{16}$ x $^{1}/_{4}$in (46 x 6mm) for door stiles

- 3 x $2^{1}/_{2}$in (76 x 64mm) for cabinet back (grain to run with short length)

- $2^{1}/_{2}$ x $^{5}/_{8}$in (64 x 16mm) for cabinet back

- $4^{1}/_{8}$ x $1^{1}/_{2}$in (105 x 38mm) for plinth

- Two $2^{1}/_{2}$ x $1^{3}/_{8}$in (64 x 35mm) for cabinet sides

- $1^{1}/_{4}$ x $^{1}/_{2}$in (32 x 13mm) for middle compartment (grain to run with short length)

- Four $1^{5}/_{16}$ x $^{1}/_{4}$in (33 x 6mm) for door rails

♠ **From ³⁄₃₂in (2.5mm) thick obechi sheet wood:**

- 4 x $1^{7}/_{16}$in (102 x 37mm) for cabinet base

- Two $3^{5}/_{8}$ x $1^{1}/_{4}$in (92 x 32mm) for drawer supports

- Four $1^{23}/_{32}$ x $^{15}/_{32}$in (44 x 12mm) for drawer fronts and backs

- $3^{5}/_{8}$ x 3in (92 x 76mm) for shelves back

- $3^{5}/_{8}$ x $^{3}/_{4}$in (92 x 19mm) for shelves back

- $4^{1}/_{8}$ x $1^{1}/_{2}$in (105 x 38mm) for cabinet top

- $4^{1}/_{16}$ x $^{13}/_{16}$in (103 x 21mm) for shelves top

- Four $1^{1}/_{16}$ x $^{15}/_{32}$in (27 x 12mm) for drawer ends

- Two $1^{17}/_{32}$ x $1^{1}/_{16}$in (39 x 27mm) for drawer bases

- Two $1^{5}/_{16}$ x $1^{5}/_{16}$in (33 x 33mm) for door panels

- Two $3^{5}/_{8}$ x $1^{1}/_{32}$in (92 x 26mm) for cabinet shelves

- Two $3^{5}/_{8}$ x $^{3}/_{4}$in (92 x 19mm) for shelves sides

- Three $3^{3}/_{4}$ x $^{21}/_{32}$in (95 x 17mm) for top shelves

♠ **From ⅟₁₆ x ⅟₁₆in (1.5 x 1.5mm) obechi strip wood:**

– Two ⅞in (22mm) for cabinet shelf supports

– Seven ½in (13mm) lengths for shelves shelf supports and door stop

♠ Four ³⁄₁₆in (5mm) wooden knobs for drawer and door knobs

♠ Four sequin pins for hinging

♠ Oak or pine wood stain

♠ Tacky glue

# MAKING THE KITCHEN DRESSER

**1** Take a door stile and drill a ⅟₃₂in (1mm) hole centrally down into the end of the wood piece, approximately ⅜in (10mm) deep. Repeat the procedure at the opposite end of the wood piece.

**2** Use fine-grade sandpaper to gently sand one long edge of the door stile until you achieve a rounded edge. Take another door stile and repeat steps 1 and 2.

**3** Take the cabinet base wood piece and transfer the drill hole positions from the cabinet base template. Use a ⅟₃₂in (1mm) drill bit to drill the holes through the wood. Repeat the procedures with one of the drawer support wood pieces using the drawer support template.

**4** Take two drawer front wood pieces and use a ruler to join each corner with a feint pencil line. Use a pin vice with a ⅟₁₆in (1.5mm) drill bit to drill a hole through the centre of the marked crosses. Repeat the procedure with the two unprepared door stiles but only drill partway through the wood. Erase the pencil marks.

**5** Take the shelves back pieces and sparingly glue the edges of equal length together. Measure and mark every ⅜in (9.5mm) along the length of the wood. Use a scoring tool to score along the marked lines to create the effect of panels.
**TIP** Ensure the glue does not seep through the join as the piece will be stained at a later stage. ☞

**6** Take the cabinet back wood pieces and sparingly glue the edges of equal length together. Measure and mark every ⅜in (9.5mm) along the length of the wood. Use a scoring tool to score along the marked lines to create the effect of panels. **TIP** Ensure the glue does not seep through the join as the piece will be stained later stage.

**7** Take the cabinet base piece and chamfer (page 178) the longest edge nearest the drill holes and the two short edges on one side of the wood piece only. Repeat the procedure on the plinth, cabinet top and shelves top wood pieces. Lightly sand all the wooden parts and stain sparingly to prevent the wood warping.

**8** Glue a drawer knob into the hole in a drawer front wood piece. Glue the drawer front, back and two end wood pieces on to the outside edges of a drawer base. Repeat with the remaining drawer pieces.

**9** Take the door stiles prepared at step 4 and position and glue a door knob into the drilled holes. Position each on to a door panel with the grain of the wood in the panel running in line with the stile. Position the straight edges of the remaining door stiles on to the opposite side, together with the door rails. Glue the pieces into place.

**10** Position and glue the cabinet sides on to the outside edge of the cabinet back wood piece as shown. Take a drawer support (without the drill holes) and position and glue inside the construction at one end, so that it is flush with the outside edges of the construction.

**11** Place the drawers immediately below the drawer support with the middle compartment wood piece between. Place the remaining drawer support immediately below, with the drill holes facing forwards. Fix the pieces in position and remove the drawers before leaving the glue to dry.

**12** Take a cabinet shelf wood piece and position and glue inside the bottom of the construction resting against the back piece. Position and glue the cabinet base wood piece centrally underneath with the chamfered edges facing upwards and the drill holes facing forwards. The straight edge is flush with the back of the construction.

**TIP** Before fixing, check that the drilled holes align by positioning the doors inside the front of the cabinet and threading the pins through the holes in the drawer support and base pieces and into the holes in the stiles.

**13** Position and glue the cabinet shelf supports on top of the remaining cabinet shelf, one at each end and flush with one long back edge. Position and glue the shelf inside the construction with the ends of the shelf supports against the back and facing downwards.

**14** Position the doors inside the cabinet. Thread a pin through a drilled hole in the top of the cabinet and through the hole in a door stile. Repeat the procedure at the opposite end of the door and also with the remaining door. Check the doors open correctly before cutting the heads off the sequin pins using wire cutters and pushing the pins in level with the wood.

**15** Position and glue the cabinet top wood piece centrally on top of the construction with the chamfered edges facing upwards and the straight edge flush with the back of the construction. Position and glue the plinth centrally on to the bottom of the construction with the chamfered edges facing upwards and the straight edge flush with the back of the construction.

**16** Position and glue the shelves back piece in between the two shelves side pieces as shown. Position and glue a shelves shelf support on top of the top shelves, one at each end and flush with one long back edge. Position the top shelves inside the construction with the ends of the shelf supports against the back, facing downwards. **TIP** Fix the shelves into position once display items have been chosen.

**17** Position and glue the shelves top piece centrally on to the top of the shelves unit with the chamfered edges facing upwards and the straight edge flush with the back. Place the shelves construction centrally on top of the cabinet with the backs on each flush. Take the door stop and position and glue centrally inside the bottom of the cabinet as shown.

# ❧ Kitchen Fireplace Surround ❧

I N MOST EDWARDIAN HOMES THE COOKING RANGE STOOD IN A RECESSED SPACE IN THE KITCHEN WITH THE CHIMNEY SITUATED ABOVE. THE OPENING WAS GENERALLY ENCIRCLED WITH A WOODEN SURROUND WITH A MANTEL SHELF SITUATED ABOVE, WHERE USEFUL ITEMS COULD BE PLACED FOR CONVENIENCE WHILE COOKING. OFTEN A RAIL WAS ATTACHED FOR DRYING TOWELS OR HANGING KITCHEN IMPLEMENTS.

**Dimensions** 4in (101mm) high; 3⅞in (98mm) wide; ¹¹⁄₁₆in (17mm) deep. Inside opening dimensions: 3⅛in (79mm) high; 3in (76mm) wide.

**Skill level** Intermediate

**Template** Pages 162

## MATERIALS & EQUIPMENT

♠ **From ⅛in (3mm) thick obechi sheet wood:**

– Two ¾ by ½in (19 x 13mm) for supports

– Two 3⅞ x ⅜in (98 x 10mm) for pillars

– 3 x ¾in (76 x 19mm) for lintel

– 3⅞ x ¹¹⁄₁₆in (98 x 17mm) for mantel

♠ **From ¹⁄₁₆in (1.5mm) diameter brass rod:**

– 3⅜in (86mm) length for rail

♠ Acrylic paint

♠ Tacky glue

# MAKING THE KITCHEN FIREPLACE SURROUND

**1** Transfer the kitchen fireplace surround's left side support template (**1**) on to a support wood piece. Use a pin vice with a ¹⁄₁₆in (1.5mm) drill bit to drill a hole partway through the wood.

**2** Transfer the left side support template (**2**) on to the wood piece and cut out. Chamfer (page 178) the angled edge on each side of the wood piece.

**3** Repeat step 1 and 2 procedures with the remaining support piece transferring the right side support templates on to the wood piece to make two matching ends for the rail at a later stage.

**4** Take a pillar and chamfer one long edge on one side only. Repeat the procedure with the remaining pillar. Position and glue the lintel between the pillars, with the chamfered edge on the pillars on the outside and facing forwards. The top edge of the lintel is flush with the tops of the pillars.

**5** Take the mantel and round the corners on one long edge. Slightly chamfer the ends and rounded front edge on each side of the wood piece. Paint the mantel, pillar construction and end supports to match the skirting board in the room setting.

**6** Position the mantel centrally on top of the construction with all back edges flush and the ends overlapping equally. Thread the rail into the holes in the support pieces and position and glue the long straight edges to rest against the pillars and the short straight edges immediately under the mantel.
**TIP** Brick the inside of the chimney opening following the brick-making instructions on page 90.

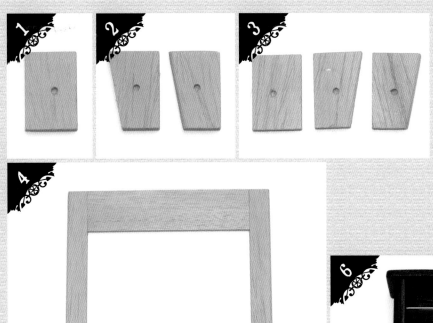

# Kitchen Range

SINCE THE LATE EIGHTEENTH CENTURY COOKING HAD GENERALLY BEEN DONE ON A LARGE CAST-IRON RANGE WITH AN OPEN GRATE CONTAINING A COAL FIRE, WITH AN OVEN ON ONE SIDE AND BOILER ON THE OTHER. GRADUALLY OPEN GRATES BECAME ENCASED WITHIN THE RANGE, MAKING COOKING CLEANER AND MORE EFFICIENT. BY THE EDWARDIAN ERA SMALLER, COMPACT, PORTABLE CAST-IRON KITCHEN RANGES HAD BEEN INTRODUCED FROM AMERICA AND WERE IDEAL FOR KITCHENS IN NEWLY BUILT SUBURBAN HOMES.

**Dimensions** 3⅜in (86mm) high; 2⅝in (67mm) wide; 1⁵⁄₁₆in (34mm) deep
**Skill level** Intermediate
**Templates** Page 163

## Materials & Equipment

♠ **From ¹⁄₁₆in (1.5mm) thick card:**

- Two 1⅝ x 1¼in (41 x 32mm) for sides
- Two 2⅜ x 1⅝in (60 x 41mm) for back and front
- Two 2⅜ x 1⅛in (60 x 29mm) for inside supports
- Two 2⅝ x 1⁵⁄₁₆in (67 x 34mm) for top and base
- Four ⅜ x ¼in (10 x 6mm) for front feet
- Four ⅜ x ³⁄₁₆in (10 x 4.5mm) for side feet
- 1⅛ x 1⅛in (29 x 29mm) for oven door
- Two ¾ x ¼in (19 x 6mm) for top fire door and ashtray front
- 1⅛ x ⅜in (29 x 10mm) for ledge
- ¾ x ½in (19 x 13mm) for lower fire door
- ³⁄₁₆ x ⅛in (5 x 3mm) for door catch

♠ **From thin craft card:**

- Three 1¹⁄₁₆ x ⁵⁄₃₂in (27 x 4mm) for large straps
- ¾ x ⅛in (19 x 3mm) for small strap
- ⁵⁄₁₆in (8mm) disc for handle decoration
- ¼in (6mm) disc for handle decoration

♠ ⁵⁄₁₆in (8mm) diameter circle paper punch

♠ ¼in (6mm) diameter circle paper punch

♠ **From ¼in (6mm) diameter hardwood dowel:**

– 3in (76mm) length for sanding tool

♠ **From ³⁄₃₂in (2.5mm) diameter hardwood dowel:**

– ¹³⁄₁₆in (21mm) length for lower fire door hinge joint

– Two ⁵⁄₁₆in (8mm) lengths for large hinge joints

– ³⁄₁₆in (5mm) length for small hinge joint

♠ **From ½ x ¼in (13 x 6mm) obechi strip wood:**

– Two ⁵⁄₈in (16mm) lengths for lower flue

– ¾in (19mm) length for upper flue

♠ ⅛in (3mm) brass drawer knob for oven door knob

♠ Three ³⁄₃₂in (2.5mm) brass drawer knobs for small door knobs

♠ Black satin spray paint

♠ HB pencil for graphite effect

♠ Tacky glue

# MAKING THE KITCHEN RANGE

**1** Position and glue the side card pieces on to the short outside edges of the back card piece. All outside edges are flush. **TIP** Use a gluing jig at each stage to ensure the construction dries square.

**2** Position and glue the two inside support pieces inside the construction, one at each end. All outside edges are flush except the opening where the inside support pieces are inset from the front edge of the side pieces.

**3** Take the top and base card pieces and chamfer (page 178) one long edge and two short edges on each side of the card pieces. Position and glue one on to each end of the construction with the chamfered edges overlapping the construction equally on each side and at the front and all straight edges flush at the back. ☞

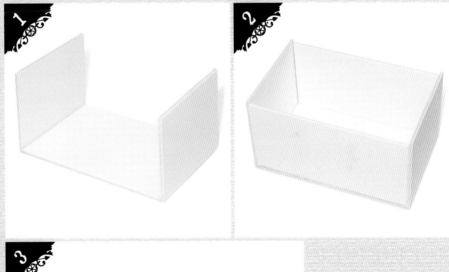

**4** Transfer the kitchen range's front feet template on to the front feet card pieces and cut out. Wind and glue a piece of fine-grade sandpaper around the piece of dowel to make a sanding tool.

**5** Take a front foot and position the sanding tool centrally against the angled edge and sand approximately $\frac{1}{16}$in (1.5mm) down into the card as shown. Repeat the procedure with the remaining front feet. Refer to the side feet template to repeat the process to cut and shape the side feet card pieces.

**6** Position and glue a side foot card piece to rest on a front foot card piece as shown, with all outside edges flush. Repeat the procedure to make another and then make two more as a mirror image. Glue on to the base of the range, with the front feet facing forwards and each positioned $\frac{1}{16}$in (1.5mm) from the outside edge of the base.

**7** Take the oven door card piece and round the corners on one side only as shown. Lightly chamfer the edges adjacent to the rounded corners on one side only of the card piece. Repeat the procedure with the

top fire door and the ledge. Measure and mark $\frac{3}{16}$in (5mm) from the outside edge of the front piece and position and glue the oven door and top fire door on to the card as shown with the chamfered edges facing forwards.

**8** Take the ash tray front card piece and chamfer all edges on one side only of the card piece and position and glue with the chamfered edges facing upwards on top of the front piece as shown. Repeat the procedure on three edges of the lower fire door. Glue the lower fire door hinge joint

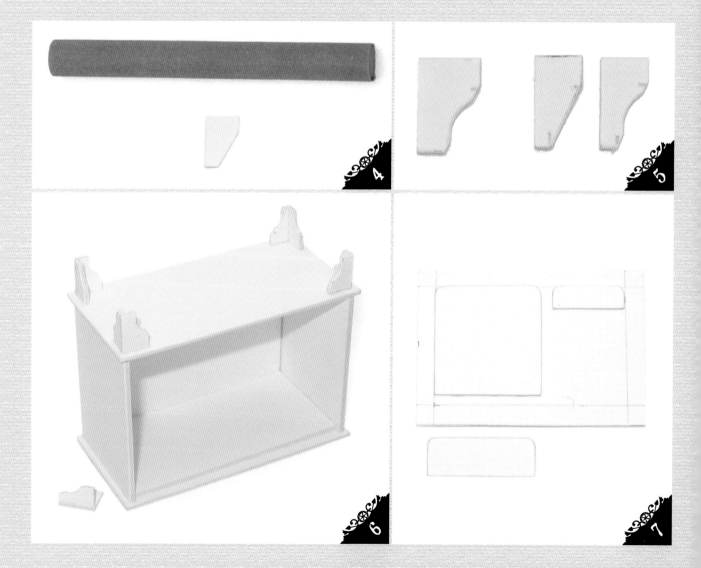

on to the straight edge and then secure on top of the front card piece as shown.

**9** Transfer the large strap templates on to the corresponding card pieces and cut out. Wind and glue the straight end of two large straps centrally on to the large hinge joints. Repeat the procedure with the small strap and small hinge joint. Position and glue the straps on to the front construction as shown with the central large strap overlapping the edge of the door by ³⁄₃₂in (2.5mm).

**10** Position and glue the handle decoration discs on top of the central strap as shown. Once dry, use a pin vice with a ¹⁄₁₆in (1.5mm) drill bit to drill a hole centrally through the discs and in to the card for the door knob at a later stage. Transfer the drill hole measurements from the templates pages on to the relevant card pieces and drill the remaining holes through the card.

**11** Take the door catch card piece and use a small needle file to make a fine central indentation approximately ¹⁄₁₆in (1.5mm) deep into the narrow edge of the card piece. Round a corner at the opposite end. Position and glue against the edge of the oven door with the rounded edge facing forwards and the end of the strap handle resting in the indentation. Position and glue the door knobs and ledge into place as shown, with the chamfered edges on the ledge facing upwards. ☞

**12** Take the lower flue pieces and glue together as shown. Once dry, chamfer the edges around the block apart from one wide side for the base of the flue. Take the upper flue piece and chamfer all the long edges.

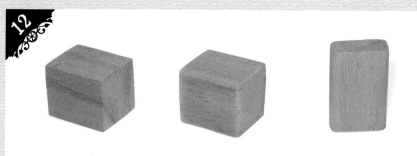

**13** Place the lower flue block flat-side down and centrally on top of the range with the back edge flush with the back of the range. Place the upper flue centrally on top as shown and glue the pieces into place. Slot and glue the range front inside the opening of the main construction. Lightly spray paint the range with black spray paint several times. Once dry, carefully shave some lead off a pencil using a craft knife. Use either a finger or paintbrush to rub over the range to create a leaded effect.

## Why not try...

...painting cast white metal or pewter saucepans using either enamel or spray paints. Black cast-iron pans and enamelled saucepans were widely used during the Edwardian era.

# Kitchenware

T HE VICTORIAN ERA SAW A HUGE
DEVELOPMENT IN THE DESIGN OF
KITCHENWARE FOR THE PREPARATION
AND COOKING OF FOOD. KITCHENS AT THAT
TIME WERE OFTEN LITTERED WITH THE LATEST
UTENSILS AND IMPLEMENTS, AS WELL AS
OTHER MORE TRADITIONAL EQUIPMENT. BY
THE BEGINNING OF THE TWENTIETH CENTURY
THE EDWARDIANS' PASSION FOR HEALTH AND
HYGIENE MEANT THAT KITCHENS STARTED
TO BECOME MUCH LESS CLUTTERED.

**Skill level**  Intermediate
**Templates**  Page 163

## MATERIALS & EQUIPMENT

### FOR THE WHISK

♠ Fancy-ended cocktail stick for handle

♠ **From 34-gauge (0.23mm) silver-plated wire:**

~ Three 1in (25mm) lengths for blades

♠ **From adhesive aluminium foil:**

~ ⅜ x ¹⁄₁₆in (10 x 1.5mm) for collar

### FOR THE ROLLING PIN

♠ **From ³⁄₁₆in (5mm) diameter hardwood dowel:**

~ 1in (25mm) length for rolling pin

~ Two ⁹⁄₁₆in (14mm) wooden belaying pins for handles

### FOR THE PASTRY BRUSH

♠ Fancy-ended cocktail stick for handle

♠ ⅝in (16mm) length of natural twine for bristles

♠ **From adhesive aluminium foil:**

~ ⅜ x ¹⁄₁₆in (10 x 1.5mm) for collar

### FOR THE PASTRY BOARD

♠ **From polymer clay:**

~ ½in (13mm) blocks of translucent, jade and white

♠ **From ³⁄₃₂in (2.5mm) thick wood:**

~ Two 2 x ⅝in (51 x 16mm) for spacers

### FOR THE GRATER

♠ **From aluminium embossing sheet:**

~ ¹¹⁄₁₆ x ⁵⁄₁₆in (17 x 8mm) for back

~ ½ x ⅜in (13 x 10mm) for grater

♠ Medium-sized safety pin for piercing tool

♠ Small piece of foam for piercing mat

### FOR THE PALETTE KNIFE (SPATULA)

♠ **From aluminium embossing sheet:**

~ ⅞ x ¹⁄₁₆in (22 x 1.5mm) for blade

♠ **From ¹⁄₃₂in (1mm) thick obechi sheet wood:**

~ Two ⅜ x ¹⁄₁₆in (10 x 1.5mm) for handle

## FOR ALL ITEMS

♠ Tacky glue

♠ Super glue gel

♠ Wood stain

♠ Round-bodied implement for rolling pin tool and shaping tool

# MAKING THE WHISK

Cut the turned end off the cocktail stick to measure ⅜in (10mm) long. Use a pin vice with a ¹⁄₃₂in (1mm) drill bit to carefully drill a hole into the cut end of the stick handle ¹⁄₁₆in (1.5mm) deep. Place the wire blades centrally over the discarded cocktail stick and bend as shown. Trim each of the wire blades to measure ⅜in (10mm) long. Position and glue the three pieces randomly into the drilled hole in the end of the wooden handle, using super glue gel. Remove the paper backing from the tape collar and wind around the bottom of the handle, trimming the end of the tape for a neat finish.

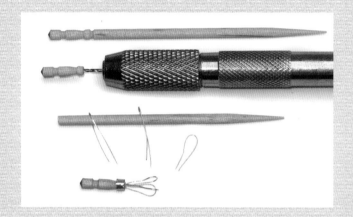

# MAKING THE ROLLING PIN

Use a pin vice with ¹⁄₁₆in (1.5mm) drill bit to drill a hole centrally into each end of the rolling pin, ¹⁄₁₆in (1.5mm) deep. Remove part of the straight section of the wood from the belaying pin handles using mitre cutters or a craft knife, leaving ¹⁄₁₆in (1.5mm) attached to the turned head. Glue the straight end of the belaying pins into the holes in the rolling pin.

# MAKING THE PASTRY BRUSH

Cut the turned end off the cocktail stick to measure ⅜in (10mm) long. Dip the cut end of the cocktail stick handle into some tacky glue, and secure the end of the twine bristles on top. Remove the paper backing from the tape collar and wind around the section where the handle and bristles join, trimming the end of the tape for a neat finish. Once dry, trim the twine to measure ³⁄₁₆in (5mm) long and separate the fibres to form bristles.

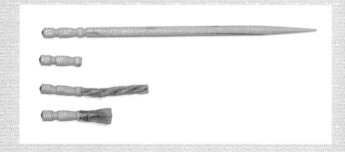

# MAKING THE PASTRY BOARD

Position the jade clay block between the two pale blocks of clay and twist and mix the colours together to create a marble effect. Position the mixed clays between the two spacers, positioned wide-side down, and roll out using the rolling pin tool with the ends of the rolling pin positioned above each of the spacers. Use a sharp craft knife and ruler to trim the clay to measure 1½ x 1⅛in (38 x 29mm). Harden by baking in an oven, following the manufacturer's instructions.

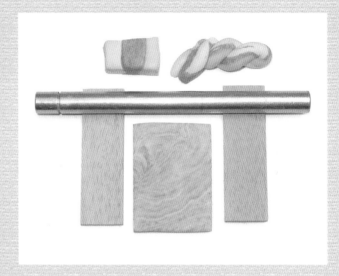

# MAKING THE GRATER

Transfer the grater's back templates on to the back aluminium piece and pierce the hole in the top using the piercing tool and then cut out. Position the aluminium grater piece on top of the foam piercing mat and carefully pierce through neat rows of holes using the piercing tool. With the rough side of the piercings facing outwards, shape the grater lengthways over the shaping tool to curve. Position and glue the grater on to the back piece as shown using a dab of super glue gel.

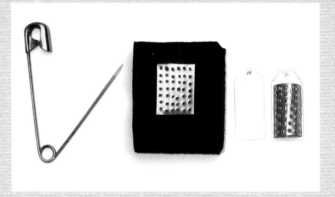

# MAKING THE PALETTE KNIFE (SPATULA)

Shape the end of the aluminium foil blade with small sharp scissors as shown. Position and glue the handle wood pieces on to the straight end of the blade so that effectively the foil is sandwiched in between and ⅝in (16mm) of the blade protrudes from the handle. Use fine-grade sandpaper to shape and smooth the wooden handle and then stain.

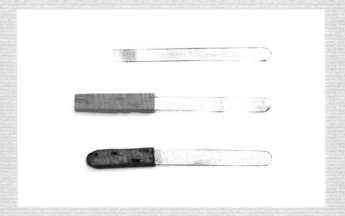

Double Bed - page 120

Dressing Table
- page 112

# THE BEDROOM

# IN THE BEDROOM

THE DECORATION AND FURNISHING of the bedroom in contemporary styles was not considered important to the Edwardians as the room was not seen by visitors. Health and hygiene were the main influences in the design of the Edwardian bedroom. Physicians constantly advised that a person's good general mental and physical condition was aided by good ventilation and cleanliness in the bedroom.

Bedrooms were decorated to be restful and light, and airy pastel colours were mainly favoured. Walls were generally either papered up to the picture rail in feminine delicate chintz and floral designs in pale pinks and blues, or they were painted plain. The area above the rail up to the cornice was either painted to match the white or cream ceiling, or covered with a decorative frieze. White or cream woodwork was common as it could be easily cleaned.

Built-in furniture was popular as it reduced dust traps and created a more spacious feel to the room. Matching suites of bedroom furniture generally made from oak or mahogany were sought-after and it also became fashionable for wooden bedroom furniture to be painted in white or cream.

The most dominant piece of furniture in the room was a simple double-ended bed without any of the germ- and

dust-harbouring drapery from the previous era and made from brass, iron or wood. The mattress was covered with sheets and blankets and dressed with a white or cream quilt or a counterpane – often hand sewn or embroidered by the lady of the house. Hand-crocheted bed covers in white or cream with fringed edges were also popular.

The introduction of indoor plumbing into newly built homes meant that washstands were not always a necessary piece of furniture in the bedroom, although some Edwardians still preferred to wash in the bedroom.

Most bedrooms were fitted with a fireplace that was smaller and less ornate than downstairs fireplaces. They were generally kept clear to allow fresh air to ventilate from the chimney and only lit during severe winter weather or illness.

Floorboards were exposed and stained in dark colours, waxed and covered with rugs so they could be easily cleaned. Windows were simply treated with a blind, nets and curtains on simple brass curtain poles. Fabrics often matched other fabrics or the wallpaper in the room.

Ornamentation was kept to a minimum in the bedroom although functional washing, grooming and vanity items would have been decoratively displayed. Walls were generally decorated with simple, framed watercolours or drawings, which may have been painted or drawn by the lady of the house.

# Dressing Table

DRESSING TABLES EVOLVED DURING THE MIDDLE OF THE SEVENTEENTH CENTURY FROM A SIMPLE TABLE COVERED WITH A CLOTH. AS TIME PROGRESSED, DRAWERS AND A FIXED MIRROR WERE ADDED, SO THAT THE DRESSING TABLE BECAME AN ESSENTIAL PIECE OF BEDROOM FURNITURE FOR THE EDWARDIAN LADY TO ATTEND TO HER TOILETTE. IDEALLY IT WAS POSITIONED IN A BAY WINDOW TO BENEFIT FROM THE LIGHT RECEIVED FROM EACH SIDE OF THE WINDOW.

**Dimensions** $5\frac{3}{32}$in (129mm) high; $3\frac{1}{2}$in (89mm) wide; $1\frac{5}{16}$in (33mm) deep
**Skill level** Advanced
**Templates** Page 164

## Materials & Equipment

♠ **From $\frac{1}{8}$in (3mm) thick mahogany sheet wood:**

- Four $2\frac{1}{4}$ x $\frac{1}{8}$in (57 x 3mm) for legs
- $3\frac{1}{8}$ x $1\frac{11}{16}$in (79 x 43mm) for back
- Two $1\frac{1}{2}$ x $\frac{5}{16}$in (38 x 8mm) for decorative sides
- Two $2\frac{3}{8}$ x $\frac{1}{8}$in (60 x 3mm) for mirror posts
- 9 x $\frac{3}{16}$in (229 x 5mm) for mirror frame
- $2\frac{3}{8}$ x $\frac{3}{4}$in (60 x 19mm) for back rest

♠ **From $\frac{3}{32}$in (2.5mm) thick mahogany sheet wood:**

- Two $1\frac{11}{16}$ x 1in (43 x 25mm) for sides – grain to run with short length
- Three $3\frac{1}{8}$ x $1\frac{1}{8}$in (79 x 28mm) for shelves
- $3\frac{1}{2}$ x $1\frac{5}{16}$in (89 x 33mm) for top

♠ **From $\frac{1}{16}$in (1.5mm) thick mahogany wood:**

- Four $3\frac{3}{32}$ x $\frac{11}{16}$in (78 x 17mm) for large drawer fronts and backs
- Four $\frac{3}{4}$ x $\frac{3}{8}$in (19 x 10mm) for small drawer fronts and backs
- Four 1 x $\frac{11}{16}$in (25 x 17mm) for large drawer ends
- Two $2\frac{31}{32}$ x 1in (75 x 25mm) for large drawer bases
- Two $\frac{5}{8}$ x $\frac{7}{16}$in (16 x 11mm) for small drawer bases
- Four $\frac{7}{16}$ x $\frac{3}{8}$in (11 x 10mm) for small drawer ends
- Four 1 x $\frac{5}{8}$in (25 x 16mm) for small drawer top and bottom surrounds
- $3\frac{3}{8}$ x $1\frac{1}{4}$in (86 x 31.5mm) for cap

– Four ⁹⁄₁₆ x ¹³⁄₃₂in (14 x 11mm) for small drawer side surrounds – grain to run with short length

♠ **From ¹⁄₃₂in (1mm) thick mahogany sheet wood:**

– 2⅛ x 1⁹⁄₁₆in (54 x 40mm) for mirror back

♠ **From ¹⁄₃₂in (1mm) thick plastic sheet mirror:**

– 2¹⁄₁₆ x 1½in (52 x 38mm) for mirror

♠ ½in (13mm) diameter wood dowel for sanding tool

♠ Two brass sequin pins for mirror pivots

♠ Four ⅛in (3mm) brass knobs for large drawer knobs

♠ Two ³⁄₃₂in (2.5mm) brass knobs for small drawer knobs

♠ Tacky glue

♠ Beeswax polish

# MAKING THE DRESSING TABLE

**1** Transfer the drill hole positions from the large drawer front template on to the two large drawer front wood pieces. Use a pin vice with a ¹⁄₁₆in (1.5mm) drill bit to drill holes through the wood.

**2** Take the two small drawer front wood pieces and use a ruler to join each corner with a faint pencil line. Use a pin vice with a ¹⁄₁₆in (1.5mm) drill bit to drill a hole through the centre of the marked crosses.

**3** Glue a large drawer front, large drawer back and two large drawer end pieces on to the outside edge of a large drawer base wood piece. Repeat the procedures with the remaining large drawer pieces and make up the small drawers following the same method.
**TIP** Use a right-angled gluing jig at each stage to ensure the constructions dry square.

**4** Position a side piece between two legs with the short edge of the side piece flush with the tops of the legs. Glue the wood pieces together and then repeat the procedure with the remaining legs and side piece. ☞

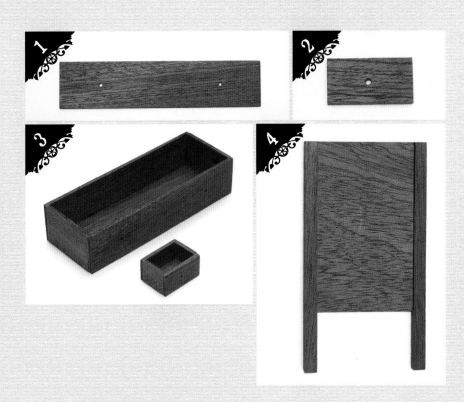

5 Position and glue a back wood piece between the two sides. The inset side on each of the leg constructions should face outwards and the top of the back piece should be flush with the tops of the legs.

6 Take two shelves and position and glue inside the construction, one at each end, so that all outside edges are flush. Place the large drawers sideways inside the cabinet and position and glue the remaining shelf in between. Remove the drawers before leaving the glue to dry.

7 Take the top wood piece and chamfer (page 178) one long edge and two short edges on each side. Repeat the procedure with the two small top drawer surrounds. Take the cap wood piece and chamfer one long edge and two short edges on one side only. Repeat with the two small drawer bottom surrounds.

8 Take the top wood piece and position and glue on top of the construction with the straight edge flush with the back of the cabinet and the ends and front overlapping equally. Position and glue the cap piece centrally on top of the construction with the chamfered edges facing upwards and the back flush with the back of the construction.

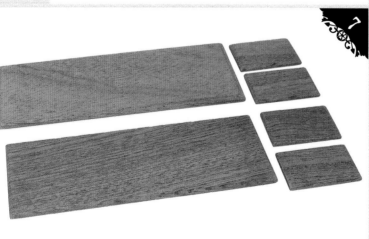

**9** Transfer the decorative side template on to the decorative side wood pieces and cut out. Wind and glue a piece of fine-grade sandpaper around the piece of dowel to make a sanding tool.

**10** Measure and mark halfway down from the top on each angled edge. Position the sanding tool on top of the pencil marks and sand approximately ⅛in (3mm) down into the wood as shown. Use a piece of fine-grade sandpaper to round the shaped section on each to produce a smooth continuous edge.

**11** Take a mirror post and measure and mark ½in (13mm) from one end. Drill a

⅟₃₂in (1mm) hole centrally through the wood piece. Chamfer the end of the post nearest to the drilled hole. Repeat the procedure with the remaining mirror post.

**12** Take the mirror frame strip wood and on a wide side measure and mark centrally along the length of the wood. Turn the wood piece over and repeat the procedure on the narrow edge. Use a craft knife and metal ruler to cut half way down into the wood piece along the marked lines to remove a ³⁄₃₂in (2.5mm) by ⅟₁₆in (1.5mm) section and create a rebate (page 178) in the wood strip.

**13** Transfer the mirror frame length and the angle measurements (see templates) on to the mirror frame strip wood and cut out. Take the two long side mirror frame pieces and from the top (67.5 degree angle) measure and mark ½in (13mm) down on the narrow outside edge of the frame. Drill a ⅟₃₂in (1mm) drill hole centrally and part way through the wood for the mirror pivots at a later stage on each.

**14** Transfer the mirror template on to the mirror card and cut out. Transfer the mirror back template on to the mirror back wood piece and cut out. ☞

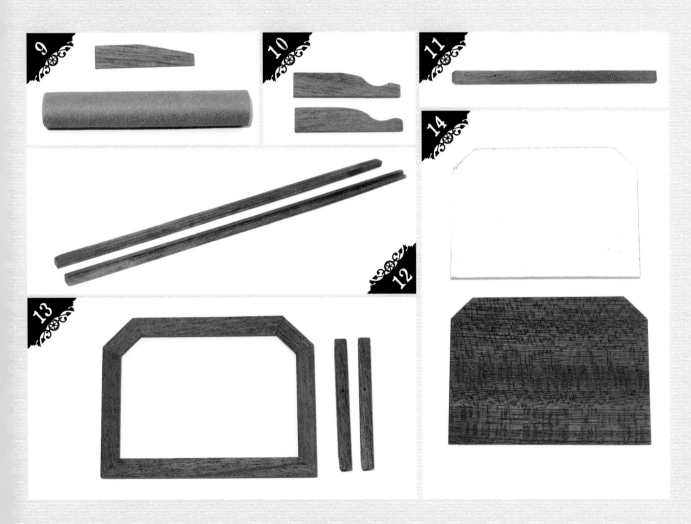

**15** Position and glue the mirror frame pieces together with the rebated side facing upwards. Drop the mirror face down into the frame and then position and glue the mirror back wood piece centrally on to the back of the frame.

**16** Take the back rest, mirror posts and decorative sides and glue together as shown. The drill holes in the mirror posts are situated at the top and run from side to side. Position and glue on top of the dressing table, making sure the back edges on each are flush.

**17** Position the small drawer bottom surrounds against the back construction, one at each end, with the chamfered edges facing upwards. Place a small drawer centrally on top of each with a small drawer side surround positioned on each side of the drawer followed by a small drawer top surround on top. All straight edges sit against the back construction. Glue the pieces into position and remove the drawer before leaving the glue to dry. Polish the dressing table, drawer fronts and mirror surround with beeswax polish.

**18** Trim the sequin pins to measure ⁵⁄₁₆in (8mm) long and insert through the posts and into the drilled holes in the side of the mirror frame. Then insert and glue the drawer knobs into the drawer fronts and slide the drawers into position.

# ❧ Dressing Table Accessories ❧

Appearance was very important to the Edwardian lady and there was a wide range of feminine products and equipment available to assist her in her daily grooming routine. Dressing tables were often cluttered with functional but decorative objects like hairdressing sets, silver dishes and pretty cut glass bottles and jars. Useful items such as hat pin holders filled with fancy hat pins and a button hook would have been close at hand.

**Skill level** Beginner

# MATERIALS & EQUIPMENT

## FOR THE POT POURRI DISH

♠ ½in (13mm) silver-plated fluted up-eye for dish

♠ ⅛in (3mm) nickel eyelet for stand

♠ Dried flower fragments for pot pourri

## FOR THE BOTTLES WITH GLASS STOPPERS

♠ ⅜ x ³⁄₁₆in (10 x 5mm) glass round flat bead for bottle

♠ ¼ x ⅛in (6 x 3mm) glass flat square bead for bottle

♠ ⅛in (3mm) glass cube bead for small bottle

♠ Two ⅛ x ¹⁄₁₆in (3 x 1.5mm) glass seed beads for bottle necks

♠ Two ¹⁄₁₆ x ¹⁄₁₆in (1.5 x 1.5mm) glass seed beads for small bottle neck

♠ Two ¹⁄₁₆in (1.5mm) glass no-hole beads for stoppers

♠ ¹⁄₃₂in (1mm) glass no-hole bead for small stopper

## FOR THE CUT GLASS STORAGE JARS

♠ ⁷⁄₁₆ x ³⁄₁₆in (11 x 5mm) faceted glass donut bead for jar

♠ ⁵⁄₁₆ x ¹⁄₁₆in (8 x 1.5mm) silver-plated cap for lid

♠ ⅜ x ⁵⁄₁₆in (10 x 8mm) faceted glass rondelle bead for jar

♠ ⁵⁄₆₄in (2mm) silver-plated up-eye for cap

## FOR THE SILVER-LIDDED SCENT BOTTLES

♠ ¼in (6mm) faceted glass cube bead for bottle

♠ ¼in (6mm) faceted glass round bead for bottle

♠ Two ⁵⁄₃₂ x ⅛in (4 x 3mm) silver-plated double bead caps for lids

♠ Two ½in (13mm) fine nickel appliqué pins for connectors

## FOR THE TINY CUT GLASS SCENT BOTTLES

♠ ¼ x ⅛in (6 x 3mm) faceted glass bicone bead for bottle

♠ ³⁄₁₆ x ³⁄₁₆in (5 x 5mm) faceted glass bicone bead for bottle

♠ Two ³⁄₆₄ x ³⁄₆₄in (1 x 1mm) silver-plated crimp beads for bottle necks

♠ Two ½in (13mm) fine nickel appliqué beads for connectors

## FOR THE HAT PINS

♠ Three ½in (13mm) fine nickel appliqué pins for pins

♠ Three ¹⁄₁₆in (1.5mm) or ³⁄₃₂in (2.5mm) no-hole beads – glass and pearl

## FOR THE HAT-PIN HOLDER

♠ ⅛in (3mm) nickel eyelet for base holder

♠ ³⁄₃₂in (2.5mm) nickel eyelet for top holder

♠ ³⁄₃₂in (2.5mm) black pom-pom for pad

## FOR THE BUTTON HOOK

♠ ⅜in (10mm) long wooden belaying pin for handle

♠ 1in (25mm) length of 28-gauge (0.37mm) silver-plated wire for hook

♠ Black enamel paint

## FOR ALL ITEMS

♠ Super glue gel

♠ Tacky glue

# MAKING THE POT POURRI DISH

Position and glue the up-eye dish to rest on top of the narrow end of the eyelet stand using super glue gel. Once dry, smear tacky glue inside the dish and sprinkle dried flower fragments on top to represent pot pourri.

# MAKING THE BOTTLES WITH GLASS STOPPERS

Position and glue the bottle-neck beads centrally on top of the bead bottles using super glue gel. Allow to dry, before carefully positioning and gluing the bead stoppers into position on top.

# MAKING THE CUT GLASS STORAGE JARS

Position and glue the cap and lid centrally on to the relevant storage jar beads using super glue gel as shown in the photograph.

# MAKING THE SILVER-LIDDED SCENT BOTTLES

Trim the heads off the pins to measure ⅛in (3mm) long using wire cutters. Insert the pins into the narrow end of the bead cap lids and then into the tops of the bead bottles. Use super glue gel to fix into position.

# MAKING THE TINY CUT GLASS SCENT BOTTLES

Trim the heads off the pins to measure ⅛in (3mm) long using wire cutters. Insert the pins into the narrow end of the neck beads and then into the tops of the beads. Use super glue gel to fix into position.

# MAKING THE HAT PINS

Sand the head of the pin smooth using a small needle file. Attach the no-hole beads centrally on top of the pin head using super glue gel.

# MAKING THE HAT-PIN HOLDER

Position and glue the narrow end of the top holder eyelet into the narrow end of the base holder eyelet using super glue gel. Position and glue the pom-pom pad inside the top of the top holder using a dab of tacky glue.

# MAKING THE BUTTON HOOK

Trim the straight end off the belaying pin handle using mitre cutters. Use a ¹⁄₃₂in (1mm) drill bit to drill a small hole into the end of the handle, ¹⁄₁₆in (1.5mm) deep. Paint the handle with black enamel paint. Bend the end of the wire over the end of a cocktail stick to shape and then trim to neaten so that it measures ⅜in (10mm) long. Insert and glue the end of the wire into the drilled hole in the handle.

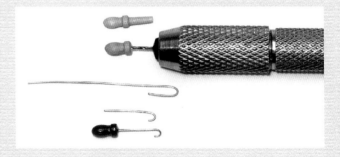

# Double Bed

THE EDWARDIAN'S QUEST FOR BETTER HEALTH AND HYGIENE WAS MOST APPARENT IN BEDROOM STYLES. BEDS WITH DUST-HARBOURING CANOPIES AND DRAPES FROM PREVIOUS ERAS WERE DISCARDED IN FAVOUR OF PLAIN AND SIMPLY DESIGNED WOODEN-SLATTED HEADBOARDS AND FOOTBOARDS MADE IN OAK OR MAHOGANY AS THEY ALLOWED GOOD VENTILATION OF AIR WHILST SLEEPING. EVEN THOUGH INDOOR PLUMBING HAD BECOME MORE COMMON, A CHAMBER POT WAS STILL OFTEN SITUATED UNDER THE BED.

**Dimensions** $4^{11}/_{16}$in (119mm) high; $4^{11}/_{16}$in (120mm) wide; $6^{7}/_{16}$in (164mm) long
**Skill level** Beginner

# MATERIALS & EQUIPMENT

♠ **From $^{1}/_{16}$in (1.5mm) thick mahogany sheet wood:**
– Seven $4^{5}/_{8}$ x $^{1}/_{2}$in (118 x 13mm) for base slats
– Four $^{1}/_{4}$ x $^{1}/_{4}$in (6 x 6mm) for caps

♠ **From $^{1}/_{4}$ x $^{3}/_{16}$in (6 x 5mm) mahogany strip wood:**
– Two $4^{1}/_{4}$in (108mm) lengths for top rails

♠ **From $^{3}/_{16}$ x $^{3}/_{16}$in (5 x 5mm) mahogany strip wood:**
– Two $3^{1}/_{2}$in (89mm) lengths for foot posts
– Three $4^{1}/_{4}$in (108mm) lengths for end rails
– Two $4^{5}/_{8}$in (117mm) lengths for head posts
– Two 6in (152mm) lengths for side rails

♠ **From $^{5}/_{8}$ x $^{1}/_{8}$in (16 x 3mm) mahogany strip wood:**
– $1^{7}/_{8}$in (48mm) length for central footboard
– $2^{1}/_{8}$in (54mm) length for central headboard

♠ **From $^{3}/_{16}$ x $^{1}/_{8}$in (5 x 3mm) mahogany strip wood:**
– Six $1^{7}/_{8}$in (48mm) lengths for foot slats
– Six $2^{1}/_{8}$in (54mm) lengths for head slats

♠ Tacky glue

♠ Beeswax polish

# MAKING THE DOUBLE BED

1 Place the two foot posts into a right-angled gluing jig. Leave a gap of ⅛in (3mm) at the top of the posts and glue a top rail positioned wide-side down in between.
**TIP** Use the central footboard piece positioned on its narrow edge as a ⅛in (3mm) spacer.

2 Place the central footboard centrally and immediately below the top rail as shown. Position a foot slat wide-side down and centrally in the gaps on each side of the central footboard and then place an end rail immediately below. Glue the pieces into place.

3 Take the remaining foot slats and position wide-side down, one on each side of the previously positioned foot slats, leaving a gap of ⅛in (3mm) between each.

4 Position the two head posts into a right-angled gluing jig. Leave a gap of ⅛in (3mm) at the top of the posts and glue a top rail positioned wide-side down in between.
**TIP** Use the central headboard piece positioned on its narrow edge as a ⅛in (3mm) spacer.

5 Place the central headboard centrally and immediately below the top rail as shown. Position a head slat wide-side down and centrally in the gaps on each side of the central headboard and then place an end rail immediately below. Glue the pieces into place.

6 Take the remaining head slats and position wide-side down, one on each side of the previously positioned head slats, leaving a gap of ⅛in (3mm) between each. Leave a gap of ¹¹⁄₁₆in (17mm) below the bottom edge of the end rail and then position and glue the remaining end rail into place as shown.

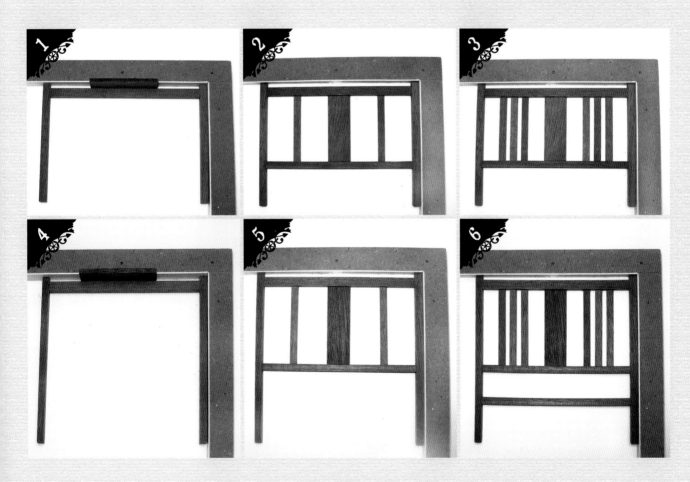

7 Stand each construction to rest on a post as shown, with the sides where the slats are inset facing forwards. Position and glue a side rail in between and in line with the previously positioned end rails.

8 Once dry, turn the construction on to the opposite side and repeat the procedure at step 7.

9 Take a base slat and position and glue centrally on top of the bed frame. Position and glue another on to each end of the bed frame.

10 The remaining base slats should be positioned equally in the gaps between and glued into place. Position and glue the caps centrally on top of the posts, ensuring that the grain of each wood piece runs from left to right. Polish the bed with beeswax polish.

# ❧ Bedroom Fireplace ❧

**E**DWARDIAN BEDROOMS GENERALLY HAD A SMALL AND SIMPLE CAST-IRON FIREPLACE WITH AN INTEGRATED CAST-IRON SURROUND AND MANTELSHELF, WHICH WAS FREQUENTLY PAINTED WHITE. IT WAS CONSIDERED AN INDULGENCE TO LIGHT A BEDROOM FIREPLACE, AND THEREFORE FIRES WERE ONLY LIT DURING SEVERE ILLNESS OR THE HARSHEST OF WINTERS. IN MANY NEWLY BUILT EDWARDIAN HOMES, IT WAS COMMON FOR THE FIREPLACE TO BE FITTED AT AN ANGLE IN THE CORNER OF THE BEDROOM.

**Dimensions** 3⅛in (79mm) high; 2¼in (57mm) wide; 1⅛in (29mm) deep. To fit in opening: 2¹⁄₁₆in (53mm) high; 1¹⁄₁₆in (27mm) wide; ½in (13mm) deep
**Skill level** Intermediate
**Templates** Page 165

## MATERIALS & EQUIPMENT

♠ **From ¹⁄₁₆in (1.5mm) thick obechi wood:**
– 2¼ x ⁵⁄₁₆in (57 x 8 mm) for top shelf
– 2⅛ x ¼in (54 x 6mm) for lower shelf

♠ **From ¹⁄₁₆ x ¹⁄₁₆in (1.5 x 1.5mm) obechi strip wood:**
– Two 2¹¹⁄₁₆in (68mm) lengths for outside side trim
– Two 2¹⁄₁₆in (52.5mm) lengths for inside side trim
– 1¾in (45mm) length for outside top trim
– 1⅛in (29mm) length for inside top trim

♠ **From ⅜in (10mm) diameter hardwood dowel:**
– 2in (51mm) length for shelf support

♠ A4 piece of craft card for register grate

♠ ½ x ⁵⁄₁₆in (13 x 8mm) plated filigree for embellishment

♠ **From ³⁄₆₄in (1mm) thick cord:**
– 1¾in (44mm) of length for beading

♠ **From 26-gauge (0.45mm) paper floral wire:**
– Thirty ¹³⁄₃₂in (10mm) lengths for grate bars

♠ Sequin pin for grate handle

♠ Metal primer paint

♠ Black satin spray paint

♠ Grey acrylic paint

♠ HB pencil for graphite effect

♠ Tacky glue

# MAKING THE BEDROOM FIREPLACE

1 Take the outside and inside side trim wood pieces and mitre (page 178) one end on each to an angle of 45 degrees using mitre cutters or a mitre block and saw. Take the outside and inside top trim wood pieces and mitre each end to an angle of 45 degrees as shown.

2 Take the top shelf wood piece and round the corners on one long side using fine-grade sandpaper. Repeat the procedure with the lower shelf wood piece.

3 Wedge the shelf support dowel piece against the straight edge of a mitre block and cut in half lengthways with a razor saw. Discard one piece and position the remaining piece flat side down and repeat the procedure to cut in half again. Discard one piece and sand the flat sides on the other piece smooth.

4 Transfer the templates on to the craft card. Score along the dotted lines using a craft knife and ruler and then cut out using the same tools. Take the front card piece and open out and fold as shown.

5 Place the front card piece with the scored side facing up. Position and glue the inside top and inside side trim wood pieces on top of the front card piece as shown. The inside edge of the wood pieces should be flush with the scored lines and top opening. **TIP** Do not use too much glue as any excess will show once the fireplace is painted. ☞

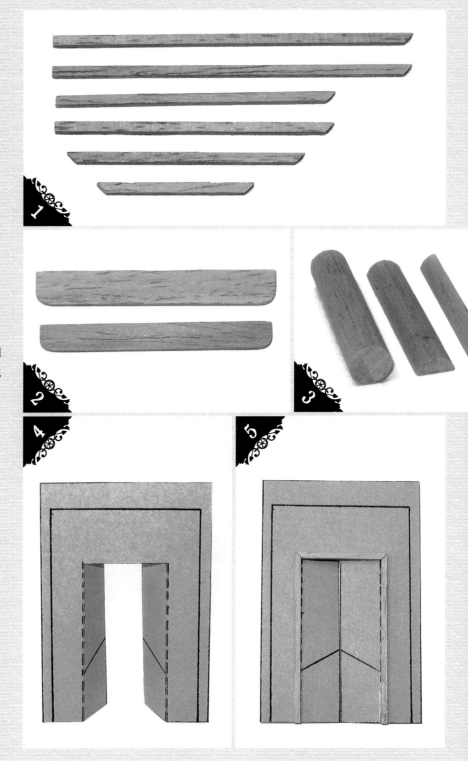

6 Take the outside top and outside side trim pieces and position and glue on top of the front card piece as shown. The outside edges of the wood pieces are flush with the marked lines. Apply metal primer to the metal filigree embellishment and once dry, position and glue the embellishment centrally on to the fire front as shown.

7 Take the back card piece and fold with the scored lines facing backwards. Attach the flaps on the back piece to the front card piece. The outside edges of the front's flaps sit neatly against the folds in the back card piece. All top and bottom edges are flush.

8 Position and glue the beading cord on top of the marked lines and across the back, inside the opening, using only a small amount of glue.

9 Take the grate base card piece and position with the scored lines facing downwards. Take three of the grate wire bars and position as shown in the top part of the photograph. Lay the remaining ten bars equidistant apart, trimming the ends of the wire positioned in the corners for a neat fit. Glue the grate bars into place.

10 Take the grate front card piece and position with the scored lines facing downwards. Take three of the grate wire bars and position as shown in the top part of the photograph with the end bars sitting in the folds. Lay the remaining fourteen bars equidistant apart and glue into place.

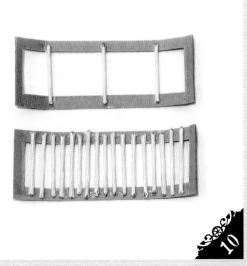

**11** Position the grate base into the bottom of the opening and secure by gluing the flaps to the inside of the fireplace.

**12** Take the ashtray front card piece and make a small hole centrally with a pin. With the scored lines facing outwards, fold and glue the end flaps on to the front of the grate. Trim the grate handle pin to measure ³⁄₁₆in (5mm) long, leaving ¹⁄₁₆in (1.5mm) of the head of the pin protruding glue into the hole.

**13** Position and glue the ashtray top card piece on top of the ashtray front. Secure the grate front on top of the ashtray with the side flaps resting inside the opening.

**14** Take the shelf support and position so that one flat side sits against the fire front and the other is flush with the top edge of the fire front. Position the lower shelf on top of the shelf support followed by the top shelf. The long straight edges on both shelves should be flush with the back of the fire

and the fronts and sides overlap the shelf support equally. Glue the pieces into place.

**15** Lightly spray paint the register grate and hearth with black spray paint several times. Once dry, use a shade of grey acrylic paint to dry brush (see page 179) the back of the fireplace. Carefully shave some lead off a pencil using a craft knife. Use either a finger or a paintbrush to rub over the register grate and hearth to create a leaded effect. Position and glue the register grate centrally on top of the hearth as shown. **TIP** Fill the grate with model maker's coal or logs.

# ⊰ Wardrobe ⊱

**W**ARDROBES WITH SPACE FOR HANGING CLOTHES VERTICALLY AND FITTED WITH A FULL-LENGTH CENTRAL MIRROR BECAME FASHIONABLE DURING THE LATE NINETEENTH CENTURY. DURING THE EDWARDIAN ERA WARDROBES WERE GENERALLY PRODUCED AS PART OF A BEDROOM SUITE, ALTHOUGH FITTED FURNITURE STARTED TO BECOME MORE POPULAR.

**Dimensions** 6⁷⁄₁₆in (164mm) high; 3⅜in (86mm) wide; 1½in (38mm) deep
**Skill level** Advanced
**Templates** Page 166

# MATERIALS & EQUIPMENT

♠ **From ⅛in (3mm) thick mahogany sheet wood:**

– Two 1⅛ x 1in (29 x 25mm) for lower sides (grain to run with short length)

– 2⅞ x 1in (73 x 25mm) for lower back

– Two 4½ x 1⅛in (114 x 29mm) for upper sides

– 4½ x 2⅞in (114 x 73mm) for upper back

– Two 4½ x ³⁄₁₆in (114 x 5mm) for door stiles

– Two 1⁵⁄₁₆ x ⅜in (33 x 10mm) for door rails

– Two 4½ x ⁹⁄₁₆in (114 x 14mm) for fronts

♠ **From ³⁄₃₂in (2.5mm) thick mahogany sheet wood:**

– Two 2⅞ x 1¼in (73 x 32mm) for lower shelves

– Two 3⅜ x 1½in (86 x 38mm) for caps

– Two 2⅞ x 1⅛in (73 x 29mm) for upper shelves

– Two 1 x ⅜in (25 x 10mm) for pole supports

– 2⅞ x 1in (73 x 25mm) for hat shelf

♠ **From ¹⁄₁₆in (1.5mm) thick mahogany sheet wood:**

– Two 2²⁷⁄₃₂ x ²⁵⁄₃₂in (72 x 20mm) for drawer front and back

– Two 1⅛ x ²⁵⁄₃₂in (29 x 20mm) for drawer ends

– 2²³⁄₃₂ x 1⅛in (69 x 29mm) for drawer base

– 4½ x ³⁄₁₆in (114 x 5mm) for door trim

– 3¾ x 1⁵⁄₁₆in (95 x 33mm) for mirror back

♠ **From ½ x ³⁄₃₂in (13 x 2.5mm) mahogany strip wood:**

– 3⅛in (79mm) length for front cornice

– Two 1⅜in (35mm) lengths for side cornice

♠ **From ⅛ x ⅛in (3 x 3mm) mahogany strip wood:**

– Four 1¼in (32mm) lengths for bottom legs

– Four 4½in (114mm) lengths for top legs

♠ **From ³⁄₁₆ x ³⁄₃₂in (5 x 2.5mm) mahogany picture rail moulding:**

– 3⅜in (86mm) length for front moulding

– Two 1½in (38mm) lengths side moulding

♠ **From thin plastic mirror sheet:**

– 3¾ x 1⁵⁄₁₆in (95 x 33mm) for mirror

♠ **From ³⁄₃₂in (2.5mm) diameter brass rod:**

– 2⅞in (73mm) length for clothes rail

♠ Two sequin pins for hinging

♠ Three ⅛in (3mm) brass knobs for drawer and door knobs

♠ Tacky glue

♠ Beeswax polish

# MAKING THE WARDROBE

**1** Transfer the drill hole positions from the drawer front template on to the drawer front wood piece. Use a pin vice with a ¹⁄₁₆in (1.5mm) drill bit to drill through the wood.

**2** Glue the drawer front, drawer back and two drawer end pieces on to the outside edge of the drawer base wood piece. **TIP** Use a right-angled gluing jig at each stage to ensure that the constructions dry square.

**3** Position a lower side piece between two bottom legs with the long edge of the side piece flush with the tops of the legs. Glue the wood pieces together, then repeat with the remaining bottom legs and lower side piece. ☞

**4** Position and glue the lower back wood piece between the two side constructions. The top edge of the back piece should be flush with the tops of the legs. Take the lower shelves and position and glue inside the construction, one at each end. Make sure that all outside edges are flush.

**5** Take a cap piece and transfer the drill hole position from the cap template. Use a ¹⁄₃₂in (1mm) drill bit to drill a hole through the wood. Chamfer (page 178) the longest edge nearest to the drill hole and the two short edges on both sides of the wood piece. Repeat the procedures with the remaining cap wood piece.

**6** Position and glue a cap on top of the cabinet. The straight edge of the cap is flush with the back of the cabinet and the ends and front overlap equally. The drilled hole should be positioned at the front on the right-hand side.

**7** Position and glue an upper side piece between two top legs. All outside edges should be flush. Measure and make a short mark 1³⁄₈in (35mm) from one end on the upper side piece. Repeat the procedures with the remaining upper side and top leg pieces.

**8** Position and glue the upper back wood piece between the two constructions with the pencil marks positioned opposite each other on the inside of the cabinet. Take the upper shelves and position and glue inside the construction, one at each end. The upper shelves are inset at the front of the cabinet and all outside edges should be flush.

**9** Take the two pole supports and transfer the drill hole measurement from the pole support template and drill a ³⁄₃₂in (2.5mm) hole through the wood pieces.

**10** Slide one on to each end of the clothes rail and position inside the wardrobe, with the long edge of the pole supports nearest to the drill hole, resting on the pencil line at the top of the wardrobe. The wider gap to one side of the drill hole is positioned against the back of the wardrobe. Position and glue the hat shelf on top of the pole supports, with the back edge of the wood piece resting against the back of the wardrobe.

**11** Position and glue the cap piece on top of the wardrobe construction with the straight edge of the cap flush with the back of the wardrobe and the ends and front overlapping equally. The drilled hole should be positioned at the front on the right-hand side. Position and glue the front pieces inside the cabinet on each side.

**12** Take a door stile and drill a ¹⁄₃₂in (1mm) hole into the end of the wood piece, ³⁄₁₆in (5mm) deep and ¹⁄₁₆in (1.5mm) down from a short edge and central for hinging. Repeat the procedure as a mirror image at the opposite end of the wood piece. Chamfer the long edge nearest to the drill holes.

**13** Take the remaining door stile and drill a ¹⁄₁₆in (1.5mm) drill hole centrally and partway though the wood on a wide side. Take the door trim piece and chamfer one long edge on each side of the wood. Position and glue flat against the edge of the door stile with the chamfered edge facing upwards. ☞

14 Position and glue the mirror on to the mirror back wood piece. Glue the door stiles on to the outside edge of the mirror and a door rail on to each end.

15 Insert a hinging pin into the hinging door stile on the bottom right-hand side and trim to protrude by ³⁄₃₂in (2.5mm). Locate the pin with the drilled hole in the cap at the bottom of the wardrobe. Thread the remaining hinging pin through the top cap and into the door. Check the door opens before trimming off the end of the pin and pushing in flat.

16 Take the front cornice and side cornice pieces and position on a narrow edge. Mitre (page 178) a 45-degree angle down into to each end of the front cornice piece and a 45-degree angle down into one end only on each of the side cornice pieces. Repeat the procedure with the corresponding front and side moulding pieces as shown.

17 Position and glue the mitred edges of the front and side cornices together. Take the front and side moulding and position and glue around the outside edge of the cornice with one end flush.

18 Fix the cornice centrally on top of the wardrobe so that the back straight edge is flush with the back of the wardrobe and the moulding is at the top. Polish the wardrobe with beeswax polish. Position and glue the drawer and door knobs into position and slide the drawer into place.

Chest of Drawers - page 136

Washstand
- page 142

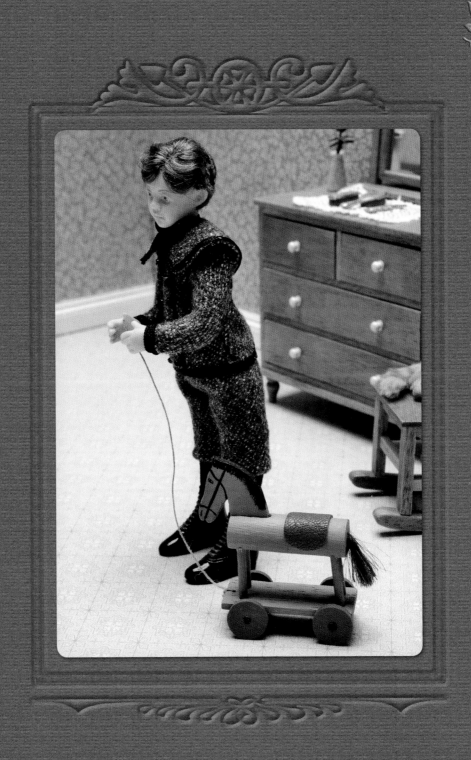

THE ATTIC ROOM

# IN THE ATTIC ROOM

**T**HE USE OF ATTIC ROOMS depended on the size and status of the Edwardian house. In large, upper-middle-class homes, the attic rooms were generally used as bedrooms for live-in servants, or they were made into the nursery wing of the home with one attic room used as a day nursery and the others as a night nursery and a bedroom for the nanny.

For suburban, middle-class Edwardian families living in smaller homes and employing only live-out servants, an attic room was often used as a nursery or a child's bedroom. The trend of raising smaller families at the beginning of the twentieth century often meant that children had the luxury of their own bedroom. Health, hygiene and adequate ventilation were considered to be of the upmost importance in how the room was decorated and furnished.

It was fashionable for a nursery or child's bedroom to be decorated in light, restful colours. Walls were generally painted with a washable paint or papered and treated to a coat of varnish. Manufacturers produced wallpapers and friezes which depicted scenes from nursery rhymes and also copied illustrations from children's books.

The attic room was generally simply furnished either with furniture no longer required in the master bedroom or with cheap functional pine furniture and was often updated with the addition of white ceramic knobs.

Baby's cribs and cots were usually simply made and void of any dust- or germ-harbouring covers or drapes. A single cast iron bedstead painted black or white with a horsehair mattress would have dominated the room in an older child's room and may have been covered with a patchwork quilt made by the lady of the house using a variety of colourful and patterned fabrics. A washable cotton rug was placed by the side of the bed on top of the floorboards which were generally stained and waxed and covered with practical and washable linoleum.

Curtains were often made from lightweight, dark-coloured fabrics to shield unwanted early morning light. Flimsy curtain fabrics could be easily drawn back during the daytime to allow as much sunlight and fresh air to get into the attic room as possible.

Although ornamentation was minimal, a few small-framed pictures may have hung from the wall. Nurseries and children's bedrooms were often brightened up with toys and games which had become much more reasonably priced at the beginning of the twentieth century. Drawing and painting, reading and the collecting of stamps, postcards and scraps were favoured activities of older children.

# ⚜ Chest of Drawers ⚜

The chest of drawers evolved from simple box chests. During the sixteenth century a drawer or drawers were built in below the base of the chest, and soon after complete chests of drawers were being made. During the Edwardian era affordable pine chests of drawers with either wooden or white ceramic knobs were a common feature in the less important bedrooms of the home.

**Dimensions** 2⅞in (73mm) high; 3¹¹⁄₃₂in (85mm) wide; 1¹¹⁄₁₆in (43mm) deep
**Skill level** Beginner
**Templates** Page 167

# Materials & Equipment

♠ **From ³⁄₃₂in (2.5mm) thick obechi sheet wood:**
- Two 3¹¹⁄₃₂ x 1¹¹⁄₁₆in (85 x 43mm) for top and base
- Two 2¼ x 1⅝in (57 x 41.5mm) for sides
- 3¹⁄₃₂ x 2¼in (77 x 57mm) for back
- Four 3¹⁄₃₂ x 1¹⁷⁄₃₂in (77 x 39mm) for shelves
- 1¹⁷⁄₃₂ x ⅝in (39 x 16mm) for divider – grain to run with short length

♠ **From ¹⁄₁₆in (1.5mm) thick obechi sheet wood:**
- Four 3 x ³⁹⁄₆₄in (76 x 15mm) for large drawer fronts and backs
- Four 1⁷⁄₁₆ x ³⁹⁄₆₄in (37 x 15mm) for small drawer fronts and backs

- Eight 1¹³⁄₃₂ x ³⁹⁄₆₄in (36 x 15mm) for drawer ends
- Two 2⅞ x 1¹³⁄₃₂in (73 x 36mm) for large drawer bases
- Two 1¹³⁄₃₂ x 1⁵⁄₁₆in (36 x 34mm) for small drawer bases – grain to run with short length

♠ Four ¼in (6mm) square wooden spindles for feet
♠ Six ⅛in (3mm) brass knobs for drawer knobs
♠ Pine wood stain
♠ White enamel paint
♠ Tacky glue
♠ Beeswax polish

# MAKING THE CHEST OF DRAWERS

**1** Take a foot spindle and use a mitre block and saw to cut off the end to make a foot as shown. Repeat the procedure with the remaining spindles. Lightly sand the cut ends and check they are equal in length.

**2** Take a large drawer front wood piece and transfer the drill hole positions from the large drawer front template. Use a drill bit with a ¹⁄₁₆in (1.5mm) drill bit to drill through the wood. Repeat the procedure with the remaining large drawer front wood piece.

**3** Take a small drawer front wood piece and use a ruler to join each corner with a faint pencil line. Use a pin vice with a ¹⁄₁₆in (1.5mm) drill bit to drill a hole through the centre of the marked crosses and then erase the pencil marks. Repeat the procedure with the remaining small drawer front wood piece.

**4** Take the top wood piece and chamfer (page 178) one long edge and the two short edges on one side of the wood only. Repeat the procedures with the base wood piece. Lightly sand and sparingly stain all of the wooden components.

**5** Glue a large drawer front, drawer back and two drawer end wood pieces on to the outside edges of a large drawer base. Repeat with the remaining large drawer wood pieces. **TIP** Use a right-angled gluing jig at each stage to ensure the constructions dry square. ☞

137

**6** Glue a small drawer front, drawer back and two drawer end wood pieces on to the outside edges of a small drawer base. Repeat the procedures with the remaining small drawer wood pieces.

**7** Position and glue the side wood pieces on to the short outside edges of the back piece as shown. Take two shelves and position and glue inside the construction, one at each end. All outside edges should be flush.

**8** Fit the remaining two shelves inside the construction using the large drawers, placed sideways, to ascertain their position. Place the

two small drawers on the top shelf and insert the divider in between. Fix the shelves and divider into position. Remove the drawers before leaving the glue to dry.

**9** Position and glue the top and base wood pieces on to the chest. The chamfered edges on each should face upwards and overlap the front and sides of the construction equally. The straight edges on each are flush with the back of the construction.

**10** Polish the outside of the construction, drawer fronts and feet with beeswax polish. Position and glue the flat ends of the feet approximately $\frac{3}{32}$in (2.5mm) in from each corner on the underside of the chest.

**11** Paint the brass drawer knobs with white enamel paint and once dry position and glue into the drill holes in the drawer fronts. Slide the drawers into position.

# ✦ Tabletop Mirror ✦

A simple and neat tabletop mirror situated on top of a chest of drawers was a useful addition to a bedroom not furnished with a dressing table. In the lesser ranking bedrooms in the Edwardian home the mirrors would generally have been made from pine to match the other furniture in the room. Chests of drawers with mirrors attached, known as dressing chests, were popular and were often made to form part of a bedroom suite.

**Dimensions** $1^{21}/_{32}$in (42mm) high; $1^{5}/_{8}$in (41mm) wide; $^{5}/_{8}$in (16mm) deep
**Skill level** Intermediate
**Template** Page 167

## MATERIALS & EQUIPMENT

♠ **From $^{3}/_{32}$in (2.5mm) thick obechi sheet wood:**
– $1^{5}/_{8}$ x $^{5}/_{8}$in (41 x 16mm) for base

♠ **From $^{1}/_{32}$in (1mm) thick ply wood:**
– $1^{7}/_{16}$ x $1^{3}/_{16}$in (37 x 31mm) for back

♠ **From $^{1}/_{8}$in x $^{1}/_{8}$in (3mm x 3mm) obechi strip wood:**
– $5^{1}/_{2}$in (140mm) length for frame
– Two $1^{1}/_{8}$in (29mm) lengths for posts

♠ **From $^{1}/_{32}$in (1mm) thick mirror card:**
– $1^{3}/_{8}$ x $1^{1}/_{8}$in (35 x 29mm) for mirror

♠ Two brass sequin pins for mirror pivots and base connectors

♠ Pine wood stain

♠ Tacky glue

♠ Beeswax polish

# MAKING THE TABLETOP MIRROR

**1** Take the frame wood strip and measure and mark centrally along the length. Turn over and repeat the procedure. Use a craft knife and metal ruler to cut halfway down along the marked lines to remove a ¹⁄₁₆in (1.5mm) by ¹⁄₁₆in (1.5mm) section and create a rebate (page 178).

**2** From the frame wood strip, cut two pieces 1½in (38mm) long and two pieces 1¼in (32mm) long, then mitre (page 178) the ends on each to an angle of 45 degrees. Take the two long frame sides and

position as a mirror image as shown. Measure and mark ⅝in (16mm) from one end on each and drill a ¹⁄₃₂in (1mm) hole centrally down and partway into the side of the wood pieces for the mirror pivots at a later stage.

**3** Take a post piece and measure and mark ³⁄₁₆in (5mm) down from one end. Drill a ¹⁄₃₂in (1mm) hole centrally through the wood piece. Chamfer (page 178) the end of the post nearest to the drilled hole. Repeat the procedure with the remaining mirror post.

**4** Using the same drill bit, drill a hole centrally up into the base end of each post approximately ⅛in (3mm) deep. Take the base wood piece and transfer the drill hole measurements from the base template and drill through the wood at each marked point.

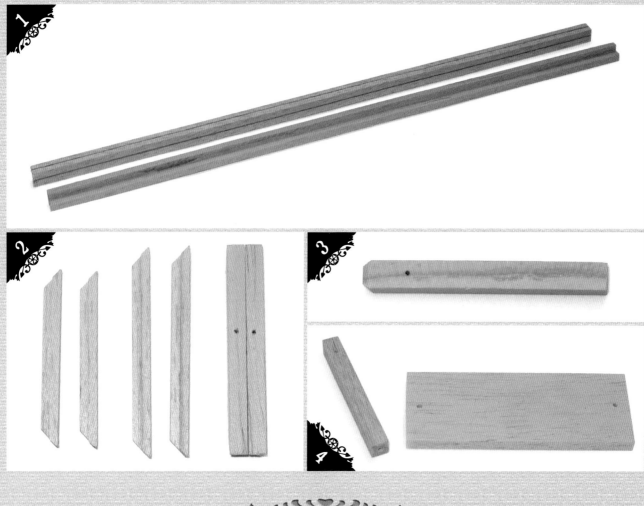

5 Take the base piece and round the corners on one long side only using fine-grade sandpaper. Very gently round off the inside and outside front edges on each of the frame pieces. Sparingly stain all wood pieces.

6 Position and glue the mirror frame pieces together with the rebated side facing upwards. Drop the mirror face down into the frame, then position and glue the mirror back wood piece centrally on to the back of the frame. Polish the mirror frame, posts and base with beeswax polish. **TIP** Use a right-angled gluing jig to ensure the construction dries square.

7 Trim the head of the pivot pins to measure 7/32in (5mm) long and thread through the holes in the posts. Insert the pointed end of the discarded pin into the bottom of the post and then trim to protrude by 1/16in (1.5mm).

8 Insert and glue the pins into the relevant drilled holes in the base and mirror as shown.

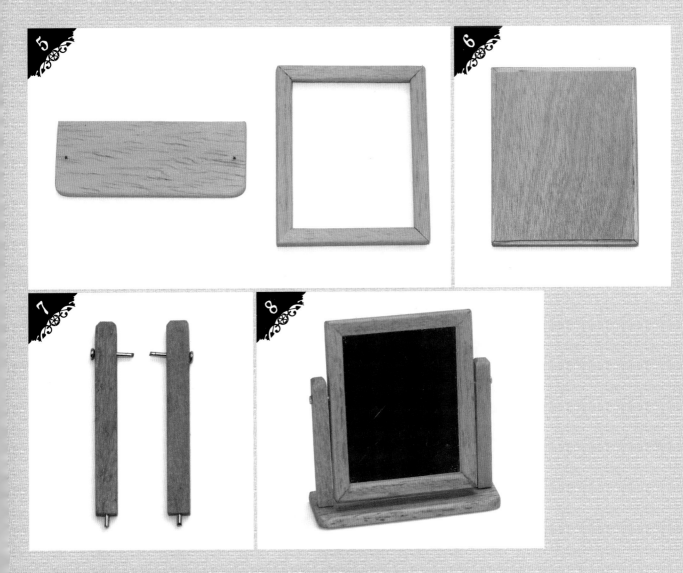

# ⇜ Washstand ⇝

**A**LTHOUGH PLUMBED-IN BATHROOMS WERE A COMMON FEATURE OF MANY NEWLY BUILT EDWARDIAN MIDDLE CLASS HOMES, A WASHSTAND WITH A CERAMIC WATER JUG AND EWER DECORATED IN A FLORAL THEME WOULD STILL HAVE BEEN USED IN THE MAJORITY OF BEDROOMS. THE QUALITY OF THE WASHSTAND DEPENDED ON THE RANKING STATUS OF THE BEDROOM AND IN THE ATTIC BEDROOM MOST FURNITURE WAS MADE FROM PINE.

**Dimensions** 2¾in (70mm) high; 1⅝in (41mm) wide; 1⁹⁄₁₆in (40mm) deep
**Skill level** Intermediate
**Templates** Page 167

## MATERIALS & EQUIPMENT

♠ **From ⅛in (3mm) thick obechi sheet wood:**
– Four 1¼ x ¼in (32 x 6mm) for top supports

♠ **From ¹⁄₁₆in (1.5mm) thick obechi sheet wood:**
– Two 1½ x 1½in (38 x 38mm) for shelf and top
– Two 1½ x ⅜in (38 x 10mm) for side splashes
– 1⅝ x ⅜in (41 x 10mm) for back splash

♠ **From ⅛ x ⅛in (3 x 3mm) obechi strip wood:**
– Four 2⅜in (60mm) lengths for legs
– Four 1¼in (32mm) lengths for shelf supports
♠ Pine wood stain
♠ Tacky glue
♠ Beeswax polish

# MAKING THE WASHSTAND

**1** Transfer the shelf template on to the shelf wood piece and cut out. To avoid the wood splitting first cut against the grain of the wood using mitre cutters or a craft knife and then with the grain of the wood.

**2** Take the top wood piece and transfer the top template on to it. Use a pin vice with a ³⁄₆₄in (1mm) drill bit to drill a series of holes through the wood piece on the inside the marked circle. Use a sharp craft knife to remove the waste from inside the circle. Sand the opening smooth using a needle file and/or fine-grade sandpaper.

**3** Take the two side splash pieces and round one corner on each using fine-grade sandpaper. Lightly sand and sparingly stain all of the wood pieces.

**4** Take a top support wood piece and position wide-side down between two legs. The top edge of the top support should be flush with the tops of the legs. Take a shelf support piece and position and glue ¼in (6mm) from the end of the legs. Repeat the procedure with the remaining legs and a top support and shelf support. **TIP** Use a right-angled gluing jig at each stage to ensure that the constructions dry square.

**5** Place the constructions to rest on a leg and then position and glue a top support and shelf support between and in line with the previously positioned support pieces. Position and glue the shelf to rest on top of the shelf supports. Glue the remaining support pieces on to the opposite side of the construction.

**6** Position and glue the back splash and side splash wood pieces on to the outside edge of the top wood piece. Once dry, position and glue on top of the stand with the backs on each flush and the sides and front overlapping the stand equally. The grains of wood in the top, back splash and shelf pieces should run in line with each other. Polish the washstand with beeswax polish.

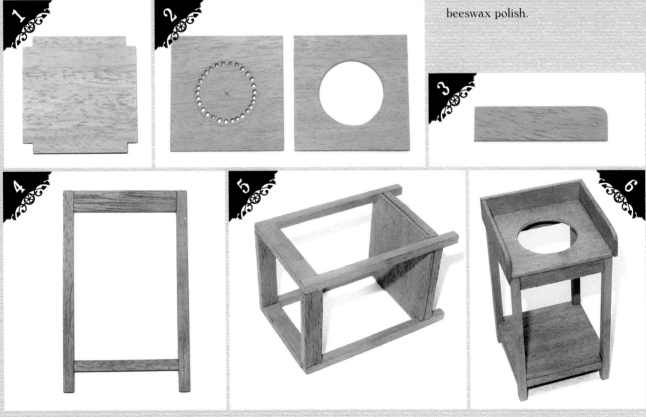

# ❧ Cast-iron Single Bed ❧

**B**EDSTEADS MADE OUT OF IRON, STEEL AND BRASS BECAME POPULAR DURING THE VICTORIAN ERA AS CONCERNS FOR HEALTH AND HYGIENE, ESPECIALLY IN THE BEDROOM, BEGAN TO GROW. THIS TREND CONTINUED INTO THE EDWARDIAN ERA. ALTHOUGH BRASS BEDS WERE MORE APPEALING THEY WERE GENERALLY VERY EXPENSIVE SO CAST-IRON BEDS PAINTED IN BLACK – OR WHITE FOR CHILDREN – WERE THE NORM IN MANY HOUSES AT THE TURN OF THE TWENTIETH CENTURY.

**Dimensions** 4⅝in (117mm) high; 6⅜in (162mm) long; 3¹/₁₆in (78mm) wide
**Skill level** Intermediate

# MATERIALS & EQUIPMENT

♠ **From ¹/₁₆in (1.5mm) thick plywood:**
– Two 3 x 3in (76 x 76mm) for base boards

♠ **From ³/₁₆ x ⅛in (5 x 3mm) obechi strip wood:**
– Two 6¹/₁₆in (154mm) lengths for long base supports
– Two 2¾in (70mm) lengths for short base supports

♠ **From ³/₁₆in (5mm) diameter styrene tube:**
– Eight ¼in (6mm) lengths for brackets

♠ **From ⅛in (3mm) diameter styrene tube:**
– Two 3½in (89mm) lengths for foot posts
– Two 4⅜in (111mm) lengths for head posts

♠ **From ³/₃₂in (2.5mm) diameter styrene tube:**
– Four 2¾in (70mm) lengths for horizontal rails

♠ **From 18-gauge (1.2mm) paper-covered wire:**
– Five 2¾in (70mm) for vertical foot rails
– Five 2⅛in (54mm) for vertical head rails
♠ Twenty ³/₁₆ x ³/₁₆in (5 x 5mm) plastic Hama beads for connectors
♠ Four ³/₁₆in (5mm) brass knobs for finials
♠ Black satin spray paint
♠ Super glue gel
♠ Plastics glue
♠ Tacky glue

# MAKING THE CAST-IRON SINGLE BED

**1** Take a bead connector and use a pin vice with a ¹⁄₁₆in (1.5mm) drill bit to drill a hole centrally into the middle of the bead. Repeat the procedure with the remaining bead connectors. Remove any waste from the drilled holes using a sharp craft knife.

**2** Take a vertical foot rail and dab a tiny amount of super glue gel on to one end. Thread the glued end into the drilled hole in a bead connector. The end of the vertical foot rail wire should be flush with the inside edge of the bead connector. Use a cocktail stick to ensure it doesn't protrude to allow the horizontal rail to be threaded through at a later stage.

**3** Position and glue a connector on to the opposite end of the vertical foot rail in the same way and in line with the previously positioned connector. Repeat the procedures with the remaining vertical foot rails, and vertical head rails and connectors. **TIP** Allow the glue to thoroughly dry before proceeding to the next stage.

**4** Take two horizontal rails and mark the centre. Take a vertical foot rail and thread the connectors at each end on to each of the horizontal rails and position on top of the centrally marked points. **TIP** If the fit is not tight, use a tiny amount of super glue gel to fix the connectors into position.

**5** Take the remaining foot rails and position two on to each side of the centrally positioned foot rail equidistant apart. Repeat steps 4 and 5 with the remaining two horizontal rails and the vertical head rails. ☞

**6** Take a bracket and drill a ⁵⁄₃₂in (2.5mm) hole centrally into the centre of the styrene tubing. Repeat the procedure with the remaining brackets. Remove any waste using a sharp craft knife.

**7** Thread and glue a bracket, using plastics glue, on to one end of each post, leaving a gap of ⅛in (3mm) of post protruding from the bracket. Measure and mark ¾in (19mm) along from the opposite end of each post.

**8** Take a foot post and the foot rail construction and glue the end of a horizontal rail into the hole in the bracket using plastics glue. Slide another bracket up on to the post and line up and glue the drilled hole with the horizontal rail at the bottom of the construction. Repeat the procedure on the opposite side.

**9** Repeat procedures with the head posts and head rail construction and leave to thoroughly dry with the footboard before continuing to step 11.

**10** Take a long base support and use a small, round-ended needle file to sand a curved indentation into the end of the wood piece lengthways. Repeat the procedure on the opposite end of the wood and with the remaining long base support.

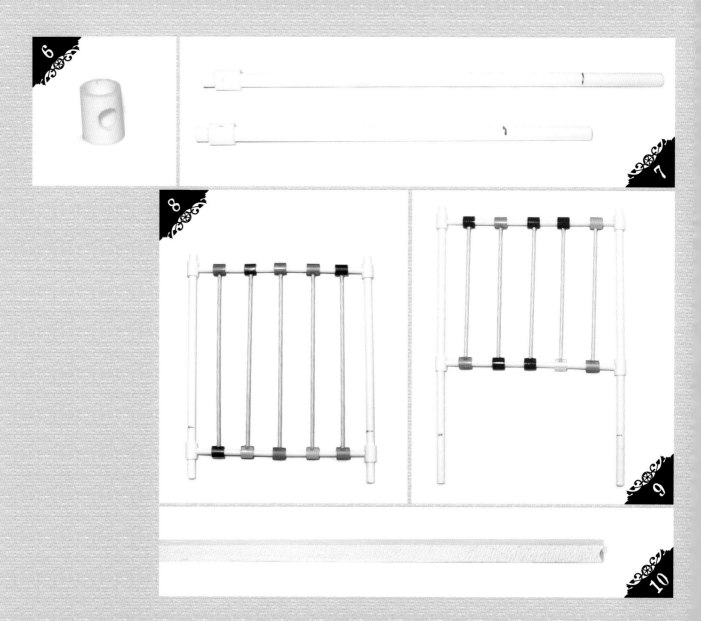

**11** Place two short base supports between the two long base supports, all resting on their narrow edges and glue together using tacky glue so that all outside edges are flush. **TIP** Use a right-angled gluing jig to ensure the construction dries square.

**12** Place the headboard flat and position and glue the ends of the curved indentations in the support construction to rest against the head posts. The bottom edge of the support construction should be flush with the pencil marks, leaving a gap ¾in (19mm) from the ends of the head posts. **TIP** Use super glue gel and allow the glue to dry fully before continuing on to the next step.

**13** Turn the construction and then repeat the procedure with the footboard construction. Allow the glue to thoroughly dry before positioning and fixing the straight ends of the finials in to the tops of the head and foot posts using super glue gel.

**14** Lightly spray paint the bed with black spray paint several times allowing each coat to dry before applying the next. Position and glue the base boards on top of the supports, using tacky glue, with the grain of the wood running in line with the length of the bed.

# ☙ Pull Horse ☙

SIMPLY CONSTRUCTED WOODEN TOY HORSES WITH BARREL-SHAPED BODIES AND STICK LEGS MOUNTED ON WHEELED PLATFORMS WERE PARTICULARLY POPULAR AT THE BEGINNING OF THE TWENTIETH CENTURY. OFTEN THEY WERE SMALL ENOUGH TO BE PICKED UP AND CARRIED OR COULD BE PULLED ALONG BY AN ATTACHED CORD. THERE WERE MANY VARIATIONS IN THEIR PAINTED APPEARANCE, SOME WERE HARNESSED OR SADDLED AND TAILS MADE OF HORSEHAIR WERE OFTEN ADDED FOR AUTHENTICITY.

**Dimensions** 1¹¹⁄₁₆in (43mm) high; 1⅝in (41mm) long; ⅝in (16mm) wide
**Skill level** Advanced
**Templates** Page 168

# MATERIALS & EQUIPMENT

♠ **From ¹⁄₁₆in (1.5mm) thick bass wood:**
– ¹¹⁄₁₆ x ¹¹⁄₁₆in (17 x 17mm) for head
– 1¼ x ½in (32 x 13mm) for platform

♠ **From ⅜in (10mm) diameter hardwood dowel:**
– 1⅛in (29mm) length for body

♠ **From ¹⁄₁₆in (1.5mm) diameter hardwood dowel:**
– Four ⁹⁄₁₆in (14mm) lengths for legs
– Two ²¹⁄₃₂in (17mm) lengths for axles

♠ Four ⅜ x ¹⁄₁₆in (10 x 1.5mm) wooden disc beads for wheels

♠ 1in (25mm) length of black-coloured twine for tail

♠ ¾ x ⅜in (19 x 10mm) piece of fine glove leather for saddle

♠ 3in (76mm) length of button thread for pull

♠ Acrylic paint

♠ Tacky glue

# MAKING THE PULL HORSE

**1** Position the head wood piece with the grain of the wood running vertically and transfer the head template on to it. Roughly cut out the head shape using either a craft knife or mitre cutters. Sand the shape smooth using medium-grade sandpaper, followed by fine-grade sandpaper. Accentuate any features using a fine needle file.

**2** Take the dowel body and carefully shave off part of the curved section to form a flat area ⁵⁄₁₆in (8mm) wide and sand smooth. Transfer the drill hole positions from the leg joints template on to the flat area. Use a drill bit with a ¹⁄₁₆in (1.5mm) drill bit to drill ¹⁄₁₆in (1.5mm) down into the wood (page 93 step 2).

**3** Measure and mark ³⁄₈in (10mm) centrally along the curved part of the body. Use a ¹⁄₁₆in (1.5mm) drill bit to drill a series of holes along the line, ¹⁄₁₆in (1.5mm) deep. Use a sharp craft knife to remove the waste and sand the opening smooth.

**4** Take the platform wood piece and transfer the drill hole position from the platform template. Use a ¹⁄₃₂in (1mm) drill bit to drill a hole through the wood. Drill a ¹⁄₁₆in (1.5mm) drill hole for the tail centrally into the end of the body, ¹⁄₈in (3mm) deep. Lightly sand all of the remaining wood pieces.

**5** Fix the legs into the drilled holes on the underside of the body and the head into the slot on top of the body using tacky glue. Sparingly paint the horse, wheels, axles and platform. Paint facial features on to both sides of the head using a fine paintbrush. Glue a wheel on to the end of each of the axles and then fix on to the platform, ensuring that the axle does not cover the drill hole in the platform.

**6** Position and glue the twine tail into the drilled hole in the end of the body and once the glue has dried, tease out the fibres and trim to size. Transfer the saddle template on to the leather saddle and cut out. Position and glue on to the horse.

**7** Make a pull cord by threading and knotting the pull thread into the hole in the platform and securing with a dab of glue. Position and glue the ends of the legs on to the platform.

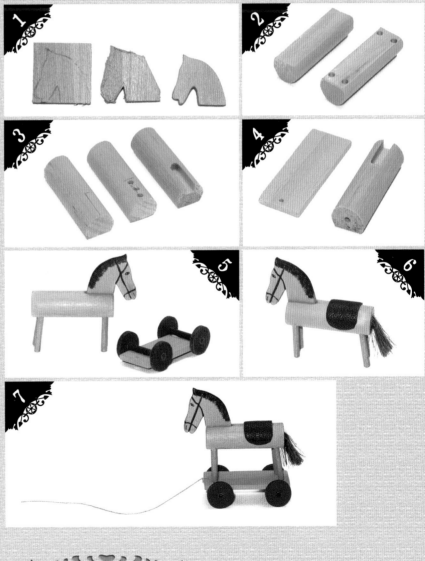

# ❧ Craftsman Child's Rocking Chair ❧

ALTHOUGH THE ROCKING CHAIR ORIGINATED IN ENGLAND DURING THE EARLY EIGHTEENTH CENTURY, IT WAS IN AMERICA THAT IT BECAME PARTICULARLY POPULAR. FURNITURE MADE FOR CHILDREN GENERALLY REFLECTED THE PREVAILING FASHIONS AND DESIGNS OF ADULT FURNITURE AND THIS SIMPLE RECTILINEAR CRAFTSMAN CHILD'S ROCKING CHAIR IS TYPICAL OF THE MOVEMENT'S STYLE.

**Dimensions** $2^{21}/_{32}$in (67mm) high; $1^5/_{16}$in (33mm) wide; $2^1/_4$in (57mm) deep
**Skill level** Intermediate
**Templates** Page 168

## MATERIALS & EQUIPMENT

♠ **From $^3/_{32}$in (2.5mm) thick obechi sheet wood:**
– Two $^{15}/_{16}$ x $^3/_{16}$in (24 x 5mm) for back rails
– Four $^{15}/_{16}$ x $^1/_8$in (24 x 3mm) for back and front stretchers
– $^7/_8$ x $^5/_{16}$in (22 x 8mm) for back slat

♠ **From $^1/_{16}$in (1.5mm) thick obechi wood:**
– $1^3/_8$ x $1^5/_{16}$in (35 x 33mm) for seat – grain to run with short length

♠ **From $^5/_{16}$ x $^3/_{16}$in (8 x 5mm) obechi strip wood:**
– Two $2^1/_4$in (57mm) lengths for rockers

♠ **From $^3/_{16}$ x $^1/_8$in (5 x 3mm) obechi strip wood:**
– Two $2^1/_2$in (64mm) lengths for back legs
– Two 1in (26mm) lengths for front legs

♠ **From $^1/_8$ x $^1/_8$in (3 x 3mm) thick obechi strip wood:**
– Four $1^1/_{16}$in (27mm) lengths for side stretchers

♠ Oak or pine wood stain

♠ Tacky glue

♠ Beeswax polish

# MAKING THE CRAFTSMAN CHILD'S ROCKING CHAIR

1 Transfer the rocker template on to the wide side of a rocker wood piece. Use a craft knife and/or mitre cutters to roughly cut around the outline of the rocker. Repeat this procedure with the remaining rocker piece.

2 Place one rocker on top of the other and shape the two pieces together, using medium-grade sandpaper first, followed by fine-grade sandpaper.

3 Position the seat wood piece with the wood grain running horizontally and transfer the seat template on to the wood piece and cut out. To prevent the wood from splitting, first cut against the grain and then cut with the grain of the wood. Lightly sand all of the wood pieces and stain them sparingly to prevent the wood warping.

4 Take the two front legs and two front stretchers and glue together as shown on the front leg construction template. All pieces are positioned wide-side down. **TIP** Use a right-angled gluing jig at each stage to ensure the construction dries square.

5 Take the two back legs, two back rails, two back stretchers and a back slat and glue together as shown on the back leg construction template. All pieces are positioned wide-side down.

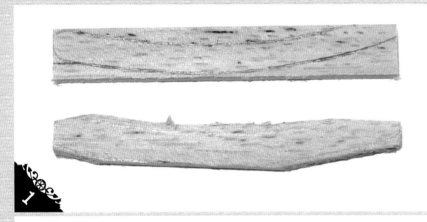

**6** Position the back construction with the side where the rails and slats are inset facing upwards. Take two side stretchers and fix on top of the back legs in line with the previously positioned back stretcher as shown. The inside edge of the side stretchers are flush with the inside edge of the back legs.

**7** Take the remaining side stretchers and fix on top of the back legs immediately below the back stretcher at the bottom of the back legs. The inside edge of the stretchers are flush with the inside edge of the back legs.

**8** Position and glue the front leg construction on to the ends of the side stretchers. The side where the front stretchers are inset should face forwards. Line up the ends of the side stretchers as before and ensure the inside edge of the stretchers are flush with the inside edges of the front legs.

**9** Position and glue the seat piece into place. The ends of the legs should be gently sanded to a slope to match the shape of the rockers. Before starting to sand, refer to step 10 to dry fit the chair to the rockers and examine the correct angles required for sanding.

**10** Place the chair on top of the rockers leaving a gap of ¼in (6mm) from the rounded front end of the rockers to the front of the legs and glue into place. Polish the rocking chair with beeswax polish.

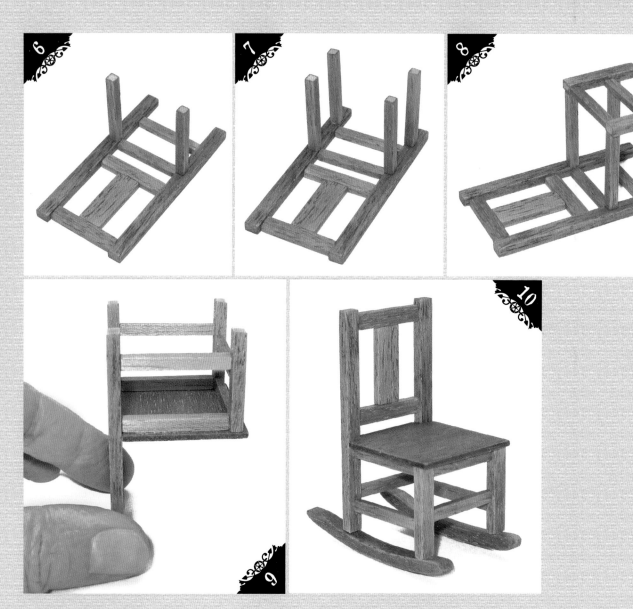

# Items in the Hallway

## Arts & Crafts Hallstand

**1 BACK LEG (A)**
A 1/4in (6mm)
B 6in (152mm)
C 1 3/8in (35mm)
D 1/4in (6mm)
E 4 3/8in (111mm)

**2 BACK LEG (B)**
A 3/4in (19mm)
B 2 1/8in (54mm)

**3 UPPER CROSS RAIL**
A 1/4in (6mm)
B 3 1/4in (82mm)
C 1/8in (3mm)
D 1/4in (6mm)
E 2 1/2in (64mm)

**4 FRONT**
A 1/2in (13mm)
B 2 5/8in (67mm)
C 1/4in (6mm)
D 3/4in (19mm)
E 1 1/8in (29mm)

**5 TRAY BASE**
A 3/4in (19mm)
B 2 3/4in (70mm)
C 3/16in (5mm)
D 1/2in (13mm)
E 1/8in (3mm)
F 1 3/8in (34mm)

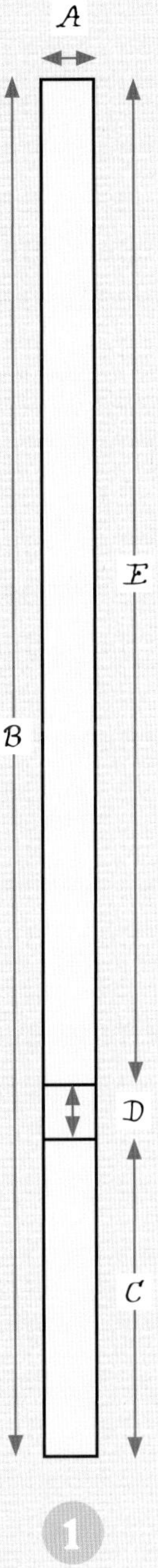


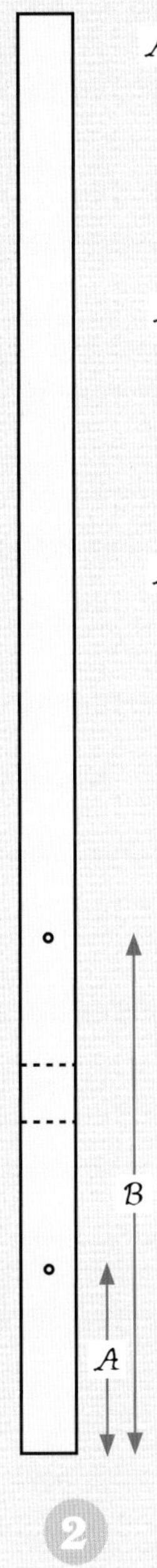


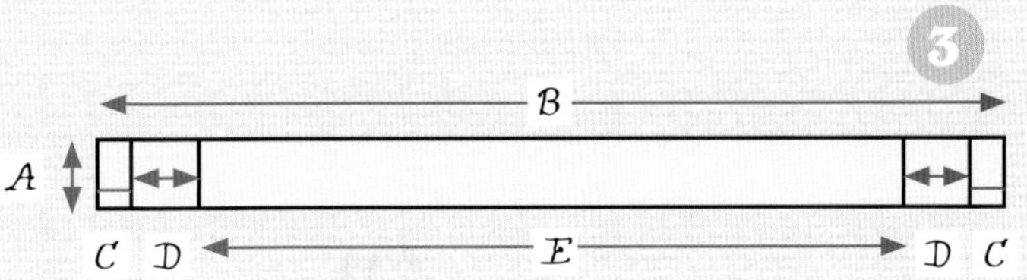


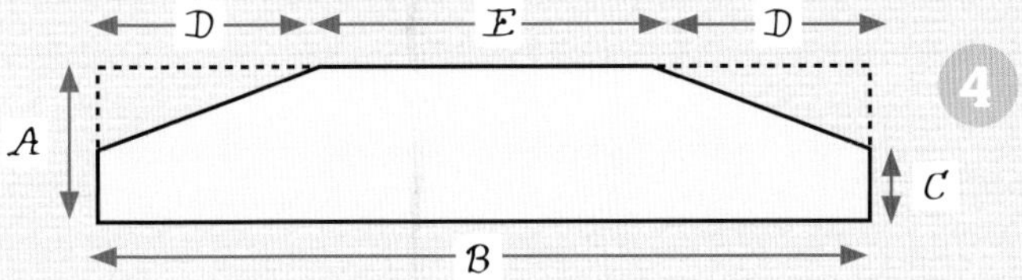


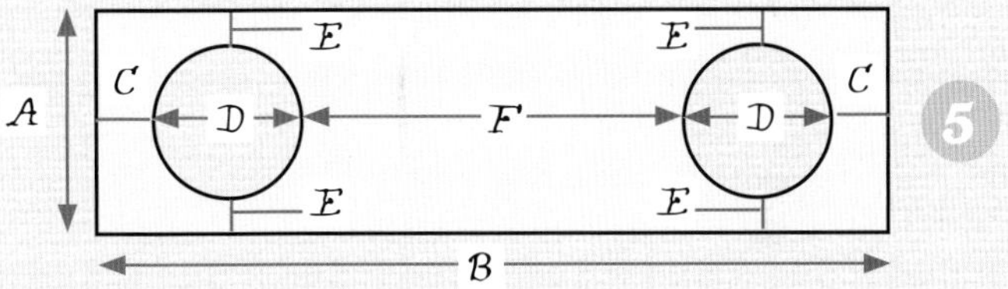


## Potted Fern Plant

**1 LEAF TEMPLATE**
A 1 1/4in (32mm)
B 1/2in (13mm)

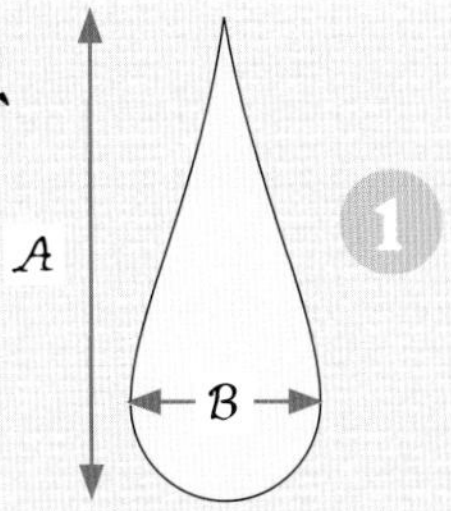


## Plant Stand

**1 SHELF**
A 3/4in (19mm)
B 3/4in (19mm)
C 1/2in (13mm)
D 1/8in (3mm)

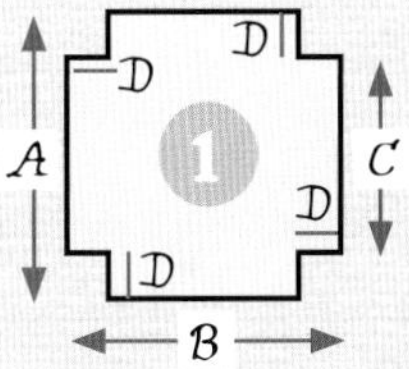


## Decorative Metalware

scored lines -----

**1 LID COVER**
A 31/32 (25mm)
B 1 11/32in (34mm)
C 21/32in (17mm)
D 1 1/32in (26mm)
E 5/32in (4mm)
F 5/32in (4mm)

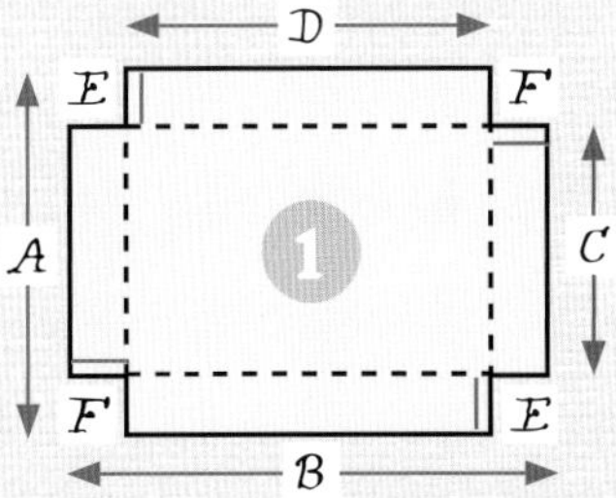


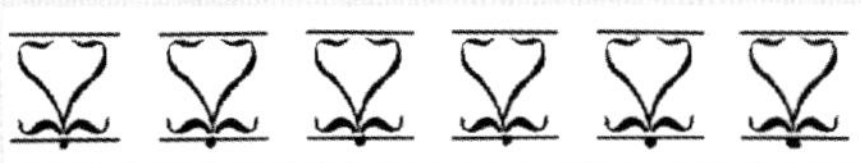

Plant pot design

Box design

# Items in the Hallway

## CRAFTSMAN HALL BENCH

### 1 SEAT
A 1⁹⁄₁₆in (40mm)
B 3³⁄₁₆in (81mm)
C 1⁵⁄₁₆in (34mm)
D 2¹⁵⁄₁₆in (75mm)
E ⅛in (3mm)
F ⅛in (3mm)

### 2 BACK
A ⅝in (16mm)
B 3⁷⁄₁₆in (87mm)
C ⁹⁄₁₆in (14mm)
D 2¹⁵⁄₁₆in (75mm)
E ¹⁄₃₂in (1mm)
F ¼in (6mm)

### 3 CROSS STRETCHER
A ⁵⁄₁₆in (8mm)
B 3⁵⁄₁₆in (84mm)
C ⅛in (3mm)
D 3¹⁄₁₆in (78mm)
E ³⁄₃₂in (2.5mm)
F ⅛in (3mm)

### 4 ARMS & SIDE STRETCHERS
A ⁵⁄₁₆in (8mm)
B 1¹³⁄₁₆in (46mm)
C ¼in (6mm)
D 1⁵⁄₁₆in (34mm)
E ¹⁄₃₂in (1mm)
F ¼in (6mm)

### 5 SIDE STRETCHERS
A ⅞in (22mm)
B ³⁄₃₂in (2.5mm)
C ¹⁄₁₆in (1.5mm)
D ⅛in (3mm)

### 6 FRONT LEG
A ⁹⁄₃₂in (7mm)
B ³⁄₃₂in (3mm)
C ¼in (6mm)
D 1³⁄₈in (35mm)
E ¹⁄₁₆in (1.5mm)
F ¹⁄₁₆in (1.5mm)

### 7 BACK LEG (A)
A ⁹⁄₃₂in (7mm)
B ²⁷⁄₃₂in (22mm)
C ¼in (6mm)
D 1³⁄₈in (35mm)
E ¹⁄₁₆in (1.5mm)
F ¹⁄₁₆in (1.5mm)

### 8 BACK LEG (B)
A ⁵⁄₃₂in (4mm)
B ⁹⁄₁₆in (14mm)
C 2⁹⁄₃₂in (58mm)
D ¹⁄₁₆in (1.5mm)
E ¹⁄₁₆in (1.5mm)

### 9 SEAT COVER
A 2¹⁄₁₆in (53mm)
B 3¹¹⁄₁₆in (95mm)
C 1⁵⁄₁₆in (33mm)
D 2¹⁵⁄₁₆in (75mm)
E ⅜in (10mm)
F ⅜in (10mm)

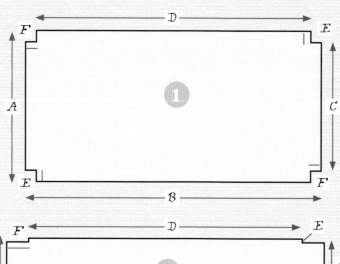
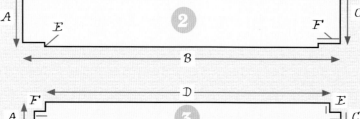
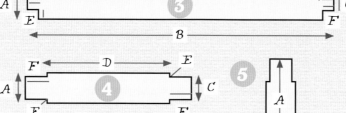
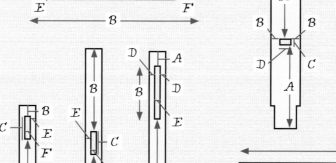

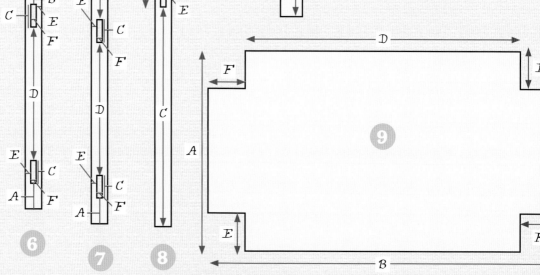

# Items in the Hallway

## Arts & Crafts Occasional Table

### 1 TOP
A 1¾in (44mm)

### 2 LEG (A)
A 2⅟₁₆in (52mm)
B ¹³⁄₃₂in (10.5mm)
C ⁹⁄₁₆in (14mm)
D ⁷⁄₆₄in (2.75mm)
E ³⁄₁₆in (5mm)
F ³⁄₃₂in (2.5mm)

### 3 LEG (B)
A ⅟₁₆in (1.5mm)
B ³⁄₃₂in (2.5mm)
C ³⁄₁₆in (5mm)

### 4 LOWER STRETCHER
A ³⁄₃₂in (2.5mm)
B 1¾in (44mm)
C ²⁵⁄₃₂in (19.5mm)
D ³⁄₁₆in (5mm)
E ³⁄₆₄in (1.25mm)

### 5 UPPER STRETCHER
A ³⁄₁₆in (5mm)
B 1¾in (44mm)
C ⁵³⁄₆₄in (20.75mm)
D ³⁄₃₂in (2.5mm)
E ³⁄₃₂in (2.5mm)

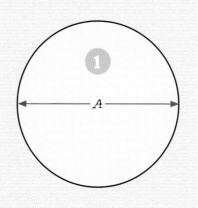

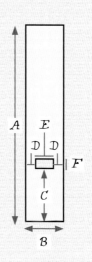

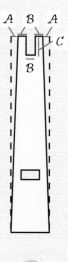

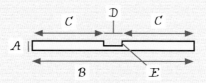

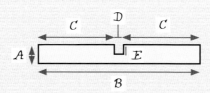

# ITEMS IN THE DINING ROOM

## CRAFTSMAN DINING TABLE

### 1 SIDE STRETCHER (A)

A ½in (13mm)
B 2⁷⁄₃₂in (56.5mm)
C ⁷⁄₁₆in (11mm)
D 1¹⁹⁄₃₂in (40.5mm)
E ¹⁄₃₂in (1mm)
F ⁵⁄₁₆in (8mm)

### 2 CROSS STRETCHER

A ⅜in (10mm)
B 4⅛in (105mm)
C ¼in (7mm)
D 3¾in (95mm)
E ¹⁄₁₆in (1.5mm)
F ³⁄₁₆in (5mm)

### 3 SIDE STRETCHER (B)

A 1¹⁄₁₆in (27mm)
B ⅛in (3mm)
C ³⁄₃₂in (2.5mm)
D ¼in (7mm)

### 4 LEG

A ⅜in (10mm)
B ⁷⁄₁₆in (11mm)
C 1⅜in (35mm)
D ¹⁄₁₆in (1.5mm)
E ⅛in (3mm)

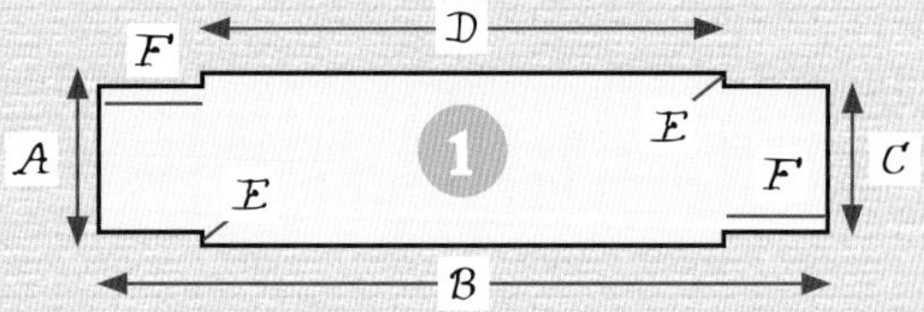

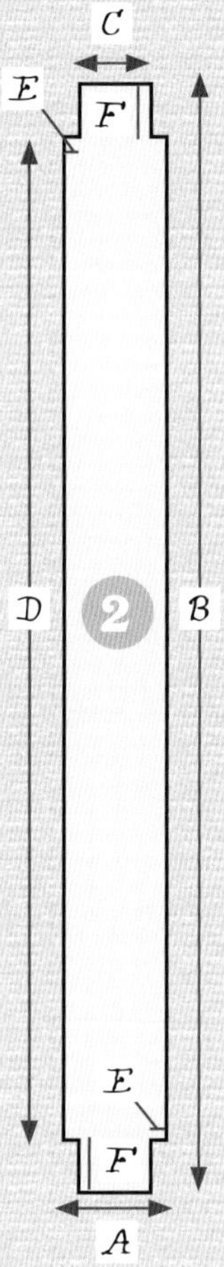

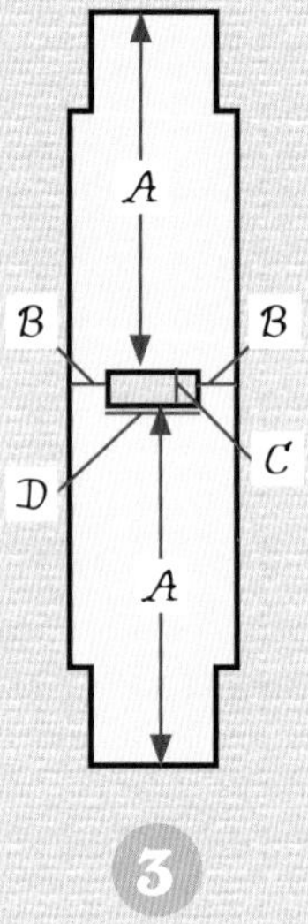

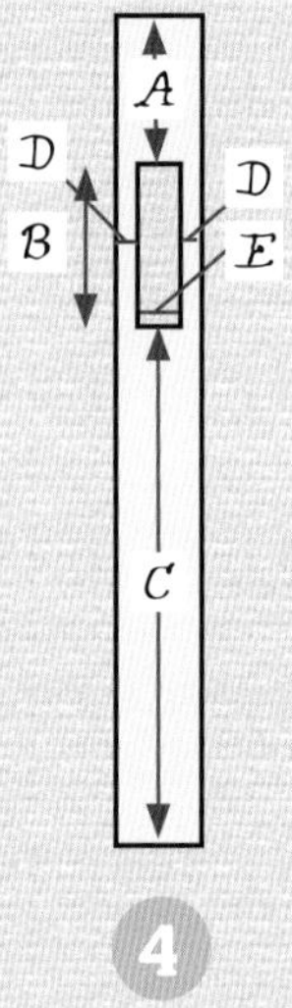

## CRAFTSMAN DINING CHAIR

### 1 SEAT

A 1⅜in (35mm)
B 1⁷⁄₁₆in (37mm)
C 1³⁄₁₆in (30mm)
D 1¼in (32mm)
E ³⁄₃₂in (2.5mm)
F ³⁄₃₂in (2.5mm)

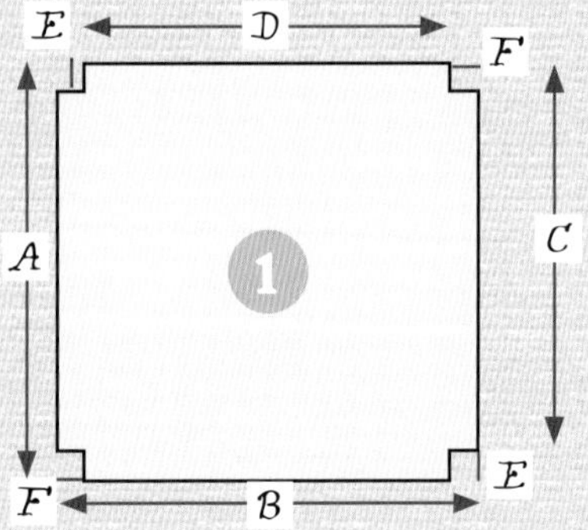

### 2 SEAT COVER

A 1¾in (44mm)
B 1¹³⁄₁₆in (46mm)
C 1³⁄₁₆in (30mm)
D 1¼in (32mm)
E ⁹⁄₃₂in (7mm)
F ⁹⁄₃₂in (7mm)

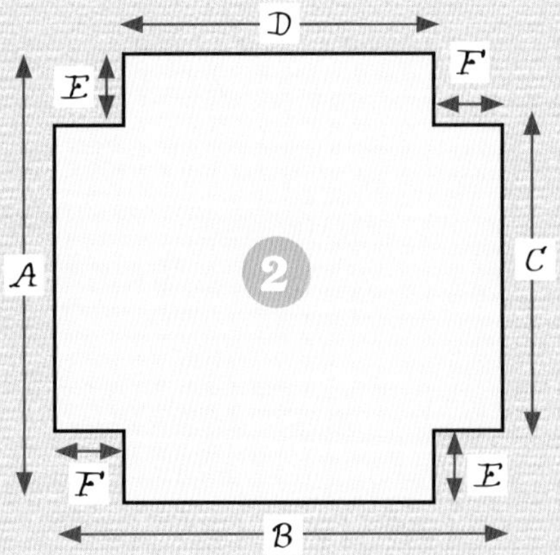

## CRAFTSMAN SERVING TABLE

### 1 SHELF

A 1¹⁄₁₆in (27mm)
B 3³⁄₁₆in (81mm)
C ⅞in (22mm)
D 2¹⁵⁄₁₆in (75mm)
E ³⁄₁₆in (5mm)
F ⅛in (3mm)

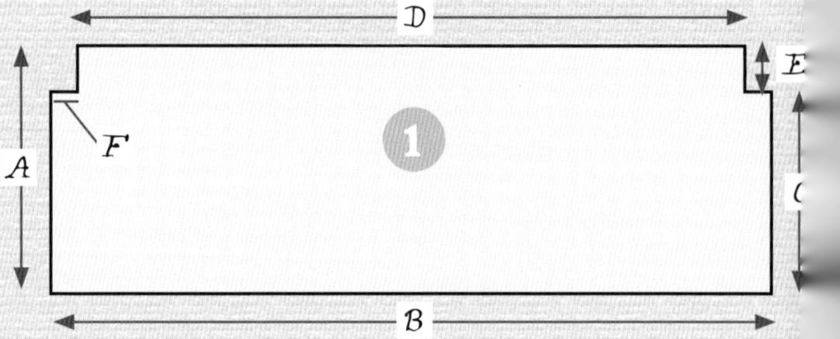

# ITEMS IN THE DINING ROOM

## FIREPLACE – RECEPTION ROOM

score - - - - - - -
cut ┼┼┼┼┼┼┼┼┼

### 1 FRONT

A 3¼in (83mm)
B 3in (76mm)
C ½in (13mm)
D ¼in (6mm)
E ½in (13mm)
F ¾in (19mm)
G ¾in (19mm)
H ⅞in (22mm)

### 2 BACK

A 2¾in (70mm)
B 1⅞in (48mm)
C ½in (13mm)
D ⅞in (22mm)

### 3 GRATE BASE

A 1⅛in (28mm)
B 1⅜in (35mm)
C ⅞in (22mm)
D ¼in (6mm)
E ⁵⁄₁₆in (8mm)
F ¾in (19mm)
G ¹⁄₁₆in (1.5mm)
H ½in (13mm)

### 4 GRATE FRONT

A ⁹⁄₁₆in (14mm)
B 1⅝in (41mm)
C ¹⁄₁₆in (1.5mm)
D ³⁄₁₆in (4.5mm)
E 1⅛in (29mm)
F ⅛in (3mm)
G ⁵⁄₁₆in (8mm)

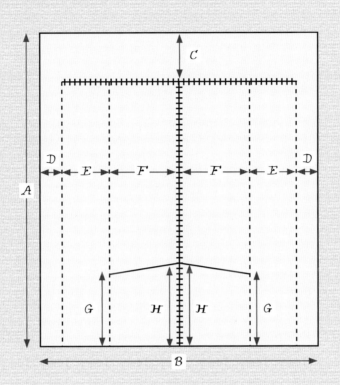

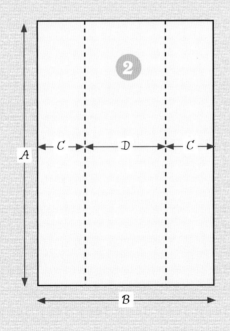

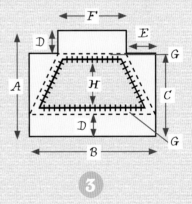

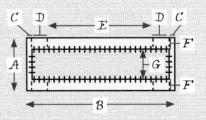

# ITEMS IN THE DINING ROOM

## 5 HOOD

A 1in (25mm)

B 2¹¹⁄₃₂in (60mm)

C ½in (13mm)

D 1¹¹⁄₃₂in (34mm)

E ⅝in (16mm)

F ⅛in (3mm)

G ⅞in (22mm)

H ¼in (6mm)

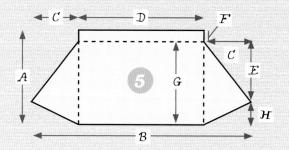

## 6 ASH TRAY FRONT

A ¼in (6mm)

B 2in (50mm)

C ¼in (6mm)

D ³⁄₁₆in (4.5mm)

E 1⅛in (29mm)

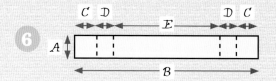

## 7 ASH TRAY TOP

A ³⁄₁₆in (4.5mm)

B 1⅜in (35mm)

C ⅛in (3mm)

D 1⅛in (29mm)

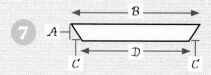

## 8 HEARTH

A 2in (50mm)

B 3¼in (83mm)

C 1in (25mm)

D ⅜in (10mm)

E 2½in (63mm)

## 9 TILE SUPPORTS

A ¼in (6mm)

B ½in (13mm)

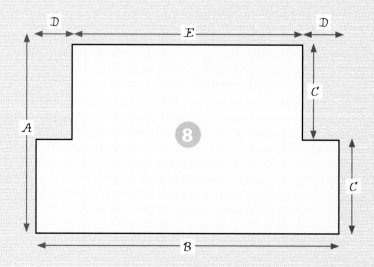

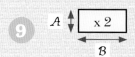

x 2

# Items in the Living Room

## Arts & Crafts Corner Sofa

### 1 BACK
A 2⅛in (54mm)
B 4¾in (121mm)
C 1¹⁵⁄₁₆in (49mm)
D 4⅜in (111mm)
E ³⁄₁₆in (5mm)
F ³⁄₁₆in (5mm)

### 2 SIDE
A 2⅛in (54mm)
B 2in (51mm)
C 1¹⁵⁄₁₆in (49mm)
D 1¹³⁄₁₆in (46mm)
E ³⁄₁₆in (5mm)
F ³⁄₁₆in (5mm)

### 3 BASE
A 2in (51mm)
B 4⁹⁄₁₆in (116mm)
C 1¹³⁄₁₆in (46mm)
D 4⅜in (111mm)
E ³⁄₁₆in (5mm)
F ³⁄₁₆in (5mm)

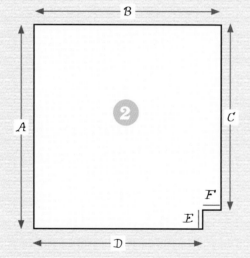

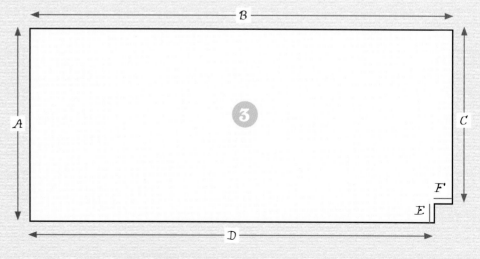

# Items in the Living Room

## Arts & Crafts Lady's Writing Desk

**1 DESK DRAWER SUPPORT**

A 1⅝in (41mm)
B 2⁷⁄₁₆in (62mm)
C 1⅜in (35mm)
D 2¼in (57mm)
E ³⁄₃₂in (2.5mm)
F ⅛in (3mm)

**2 DESK DRAWER FRONT**

A ²³⁄₆₄in (9mm)
B 2⁷⁄₃₂in (56mm)
C ⅜in (10mm)
D ³⁄₁₆in (4.5mm)

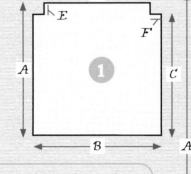

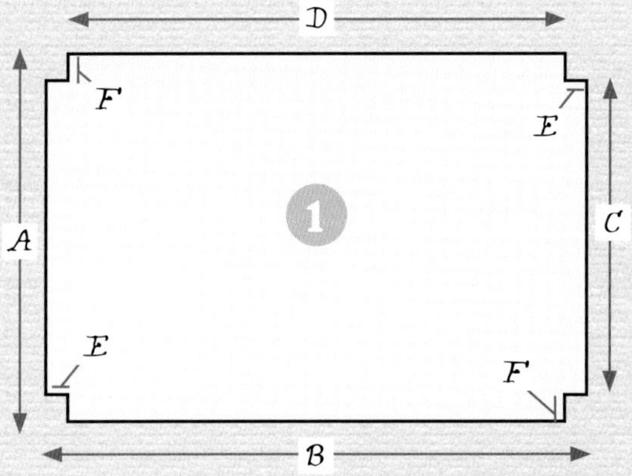

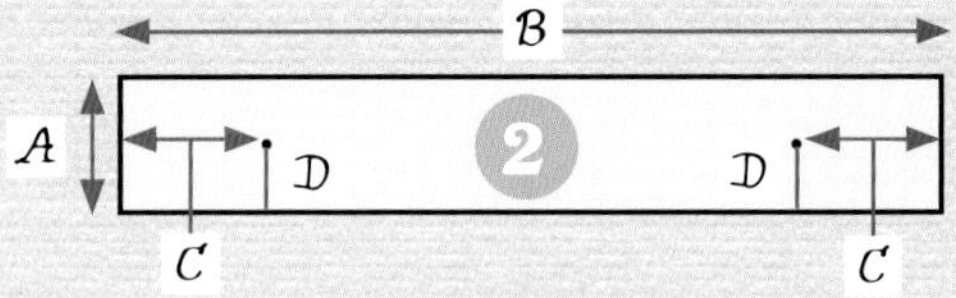

## Arts & Crafts Desk Chair

**1 DESK CHAIR SEAT**

A 1⅜in (35mm)
B 1⅜in (35mm)
C 1¼in (32mm)
D 1⅛in (29mm)
E ⅛in (3mm)
F ⅛in (3mm)

**2 DESK CHAIR LEG CONSTRUCTION**

A 3¼in (82mm)
B 1⅜in (35mm)
C ⅛in (3mm)
D 1⅜in (35mm)

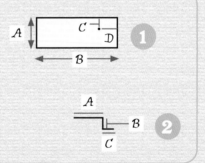

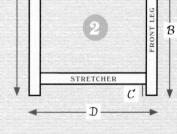

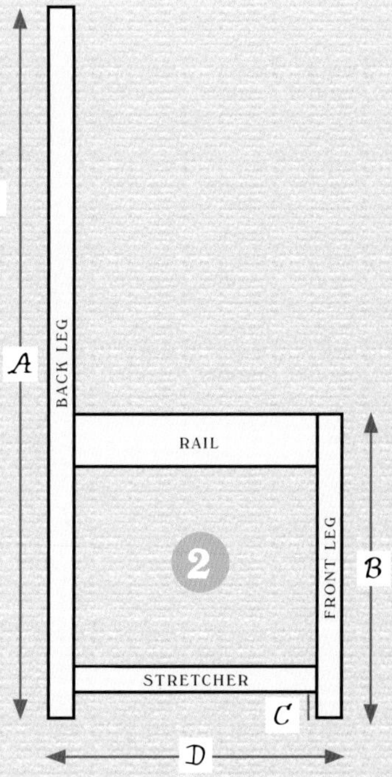

## Gramophone

**1 SIDE**

A ⁵⁄₁₆in (8mm)
B ⅞in (22mm)
C ⅛in (3mm)
D ³⁄₁₆in (5mm)

**2 HANDLE**

A ⁵⁄₁₆in (8mm)
B ⅛in (3mm)
C ⅛in (3mm)

## Arts & Crafts Gramophone Table

**1 SHELF**

A 1¼in (31mm)
B 1¼in (31mm)
C 1in (25mm)
D 1in (25mm)
E ⅛in (3mm)
F ⅛in (3mm)

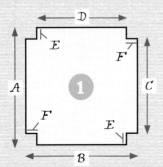

## Wall Shelves

**1 TOP BOARD**

A ½in (13mm)          C ¼in (6mm)
B 2¾in (70mm)         D 1⅜in (35mm)

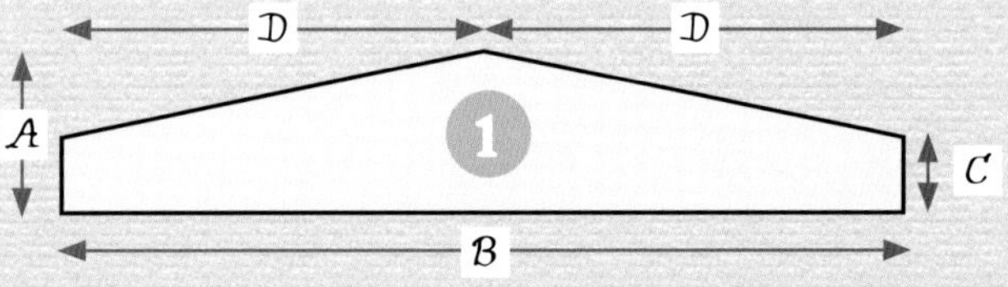

# ITEMS IN THE KITCHEN

## KITCHEN TABLE

### 1 DRAWER SUPPORT

A 1⅞in (48mm)
B 3½in (89mm)
C 1½in (38mm)
D 3⅛in (79mm)
E ³⁄₁₆in (5mm)
F ³⁄₁₆in (5mm)

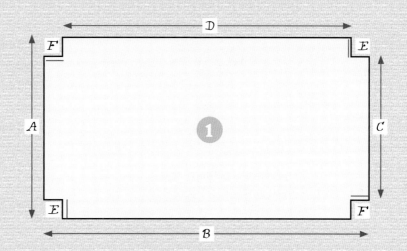

### 2 DRAWER FRONT

A ¹¹⁄₃₂in (9mm)
B 1¹⁵⁄₃₂in (37mm)
C ³⁄₁₆in (4.5mm)
D ⁵⁄₁₆in (8mm)

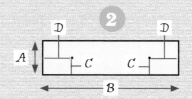

## SINK AND DRAINING BOARD

### 1 SINK BASE

A 1¼in (32mm)
B 1¾in (44mm)
C ⅝in (16mm)
D ½in (13mm)

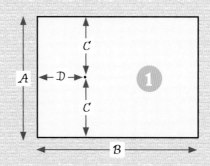

### 2 DRAINING BOARD BASE

A 1⅜ in (35mm)
B 2¼in (57mm)
C ³⁄₁₆in (5.5mm)
D ¹⁄₁₆in (1.5mm)
E ⅛in (3mm)

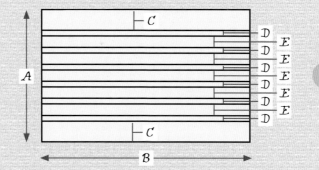

# Items in the Kitchen

## Kitchen Dresser

**1 CABINET BASE**
A 1⁷⁄₁₆in (37mm)
B 4in (102mm)
C ⅛in (3mm)
D ⁵⁄₁₆in (8mm)

**2 DRAWER SUPPORT**
A 1¼in (32mm)
B 3⅝in (92mm)
C ¹⁄₁₆in (1.5mm)
D ⅛in (3mm)

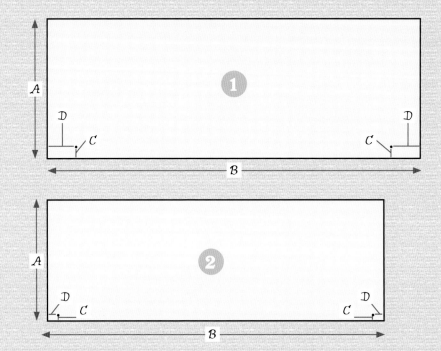

## Kitchen Fireplace Surround

**1 SUPPORT – LEFT SIDE (1)**
A ¾in (19mm)
B ½in (13mm)
C ⅜in (9.5mm)
D ⁹⁄₃₂in (7mm)
E ⁷⁄₃₂in (6mm)

**3 SUPPORT – RIGHT SIDE (1)**
A ¾in (19mm)
B ½in (13mm)
C ⅜in (9.5mm)
D ⁷⁄₃₂in (6mm)
E ⁹⁄₃₂in (7mm)

**2 SUPPORT – LEFT SIDE (2)**
A ¾in (19mm)
B ⅛in (3mm)
C ⅜in (10mm)
D ⁷⁄₃₂in (6mm)

**4 SUPPORT – RIGHT SIDE (2)**
A ¾in (19mm)
B ⅜in (10mm)
C ⅛in (3mm)
D ⁷⁄₃₂in (6mm)

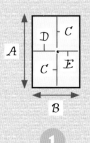
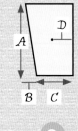
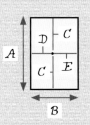
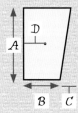

# ITEMS IN THE KITCHEN

## KITCHEN RANGE

### 1 FRONT FEET
A ⅜in (10mm)
B ¼in (6mm)
C ⅛in (3mm)
D ⅛in (3mm)
E ⅛in (3mm)
F ¼in (7mm)

### 2 SIDE FEET
A ⅜in (10mm)
B ³⁄₁₆in (4.5mm)
C ¹⁄₁₆in (1.5mm)
D ⅛in (3mm)
E ⅛in (3mm)
F ¼in (7mm)

### 3 LARGE STRAP
A ⁵⁄₃₂in (4mm)
B 1¹⁄₁₆in (27mm)
C ⁹⁄₁₆in (14mm)
D ½in (13mm)
E ⁵⁄₆₄in (2mm)

### 4 SMALL STRAP
A ⅛in (3mm)
B ¾in (19mm)
C ⅜in (9.5mm)
D ⅜in (9.5mm)
E ¹⁄₁₆in (1.5mm)

### 5 TOP FIRE DOOR
A ¼in (6mm)
B ¾in (19mm)
C ⅛in (3mm)
D ³⁄₃₂in (2.5mm)

### 6 LOWER FIRE DOOR
A ½in (13mm)
B ¾in (19mm)
C ³⁄₃₂in (2.5mm)
D ⅜in (9.5mm)

### 7 ASH TRAY FRONT
A ¼in (6mm)
B ¾in (19mm)
C ⅛in (3mm)
D ⅜in (9.5mm)

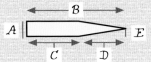
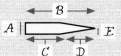

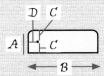
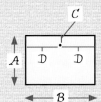
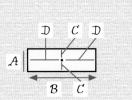

## KITCHENWARE

### 1 GRATER BACK
A ¹¹⁄₁₆in (17mm)
B ⁵⁄₁₆in (8mm)
C ¹⁄₁₆in (1.5mm)
D ⁵⁄₃₂in (4mm)

### 2 GRATER BACK
A ¹¹⁄₁₆in (17mm)
B ⁵⁄₁₆in (8mm)
C ⅛in (3mm)
D ⁹⁄₁₆in (14mm)
E ³⁄₃₂in (2.5mm)
F ⅛in (3mm)

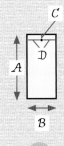

# Items in the Bedroom

## Dressing Table

### 1 LARGE DRAWER FRONT

A $^{11}/_{16}$in (17mm)

B $3^3/_{32}$in (78mm)

C $^{11}/_{32}$in (8.5mm)

D $^5/_8$in (16mm)

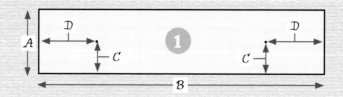

### 2 DECORATIVE SIDE

A $^5/_{16}$in (8mm)

B $1^1/_2$in (38mm)

C $^3/_{16}$in (5mm)

D $^{11}/_{16}$in (17mm)

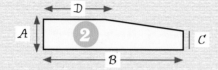

### 3 MIRROR FRAME SURROUND

A $1^3/_8$in (35mm)

B $2^1/_4$in (57mm)

C $1^5/_8$in (41mm)

D $^{15}/_{32}$in (12mm)

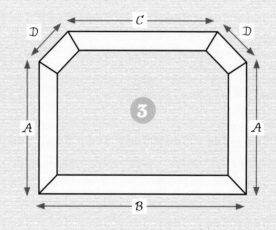

### 4 MIRROR FRAME SURROUND - ANGLES

A 45 degrees angle

B 67.5 degrees angle

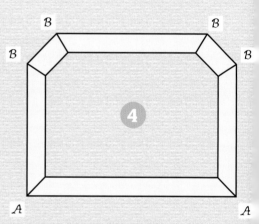

### 5 MIRROR

A $1^9/_{16}$in (40mm)

B $2^1/_{16}$in (52mm)

C $1^1/_4$in (32mm)

D $^1/_4$in (6mm)

E $1^9/_{16}$in (40mm)

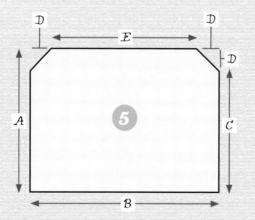

### 6 MIRROR BACK

A $1^5/_8$in (42mm)

B $2^1/_8$in (54mm)

C $1^5/_{16}$in (34mm)

D $^1/_4$in (6mm)

E $1^5/_8$in (42mm)

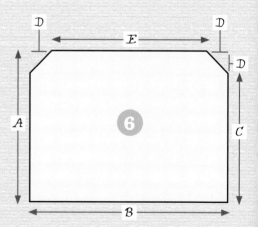

# ITEMS IN THE BEDROOM

## BEDROOM FIREPLACE

### 1 FIRE FRONT

cut ┼┼┼┼┼┼┼┼

score ┄┄┄┄┄┄

### 1 FRONT

A 3in (76mm)
B 2in (51mm)
C ⁵⁄₁₆in (8mm)
D ⅛in (3mm)
E ⅜in (9.5mm)
F ½in (13mm)
G ¹¹⁄₁₆in (17mm)
H ⅝in (16mm)
I ⅞in (22mm)
J 2in (51mm)

### 2 BACK

A 2in (51mm)
B 1½in (38mm)
C ⁷⁄₁₆in (11mm)
D ⅝in (16mm)

### 3 GRATE BASE

A ¹³⁄₁₆in (21mm)
B 1in (25mm)
C ⅝in (16mm)
D ³⁄₁₆in (5mm)
E ³⁄₁₆in (4.5mm)
F ⅝in (16mm)
G ¹⁄₁₆in (1.5mm)
H ⁵⁄₁₆in (8mm)
I ³⁄₁₆in (5mm)

### 4 GRATE FRONT

A ⁷⁄₁₆in (11mm)
B 1³⁄₁₆in (30mm)
C ¹⁄₁₆in (1.5mm)
D ³⁄₁₆in (5mm)
E ¹¹⁄₁₆in (17mm)
F ¹⁄₁₆in (1.5mm)
G ⁵⁄₁₆in (8mm)

### 5 ASH TRAY FRONT

A ³⁄₁₆in (5mm)
B 1⁹⁄₁₆in (39mm)
C ¼in (6mm)
D ³⁄₁₆in (5mm)
E ¹¹⁄₁₆in (17mm)

### 6 ASH TRAY TOP

A ⅛in (3mm)
B 1in (25mm)
C ⁵⁄₃₂in (4mm)
D ¹¹⁄₁₆in (17mm)

### 7 HEARTH

A 1⅛in (29mm)
B 2³⁄₁₆in (55mm)
C ⅝in (16mm)
D ⁹⁄₁₆in (14mm)
E ½in (13mm)
F 1¹⁄₁₆in (27mm)

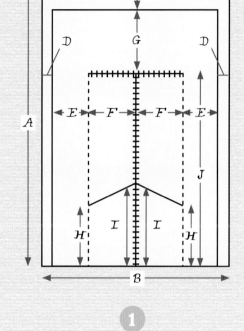

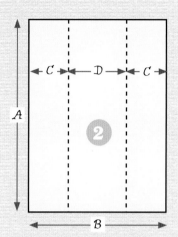

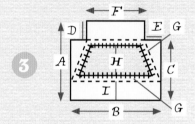

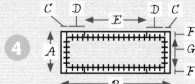

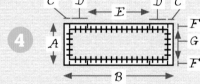

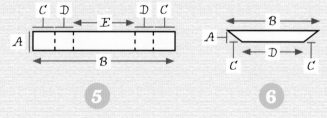

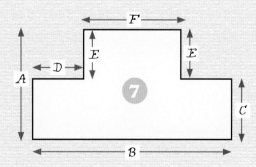

# Items in the Bedroom

## WARDROBE

### 1 DRAWER FRONT

A $^{25}/_{32}$in (20mm)

B 2$^{27}/_{32}$in (72mm)

C $^{3}/_{8}$in (10mm)

D $^{1}/_{2}$in (13mm)

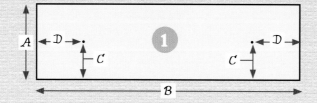

### 2 CAP

A 1$^{1}/_{2}$in (38mm)

B 3$^{3}/_{8}$in (86mm)

C $^{3}/_{16}$in (4.5mm)

D $^{7}/_{8}$in (22mm)

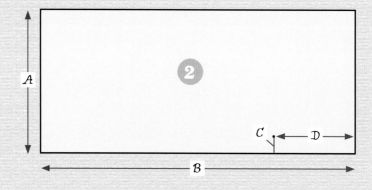

### 3 POLE SUPPORT

A $^{3}/_{8}$in (10mm)

B 1in (25mm)

C $^{1}/_{8}$ in (3mm)

D $^{7}/_{16}$in (11mm)

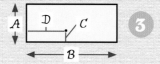

# ITEMS IN THE ATTIC ROOM

## CHEST OF DRAWERS

### 1 LARGE DRAWER FRONT

A $^{39}\!/_{64}$in (15mm)

B 3in (76mm)

C $^{5}\!/_{16}$in (8mm)

D $^{23}\!/_{32}$in (18.5mm)

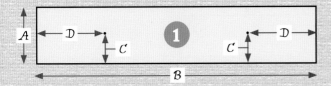

## TABLETOP MIRROR

### 1 BASE

A $^{5}\!/_{8}$in (16mm)

B 1$^{5}\!/_{8}$in (41mm)

C $^{5}\!/_{16}$in (8mm)

D $^{3}\!/_{32}$in (2.5mm)

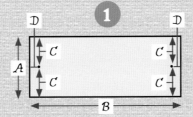

## WASHSTAND

### 1 SHELF

A 1$^{1}\!/_{2}$in (38mm)

B 1$^{1}\!/_{2}$in (38mm)

C 1$^{1}\!/_{4}$in (32mm)

D $^{1}\!/_{8}$in (3mm)

E $^{1}\!/_{8}$in (3mm)

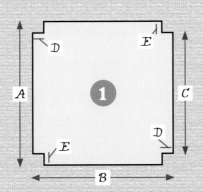

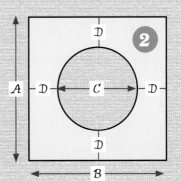

### 2 TOP

A 1$^{1}\!/_{2}$in (38mm)

B 1$^{1}\!/_{2}$in (38mm)

C $^{7}\!/_{8}$in (22mm)

D $^{5}\!/_{16}$in (8mm)

# ITEMS IN THE ATTIC ROOM

## PULL HORSE

### 1 HEAD
A ¹¹⁄₁₆in (17mm)
B ¹¹⁄₁₆in (17mm)

### 2 LEG JOINTS
A ⁵⁄₁₆in (8mm)
B 1⅛in (29mm)
C ¹⁄₃₂in (1mm)
D ⅛in (3mm)

### 3 PLATFORM
A ½in (13mm)
B 1¼in (32mm)
C ¼in (6.5mm)
D ¹⁄₁₆in (1.5mm)

### 4 SADDLE
A ⅜in (10mm)
B ¾in (19mm)

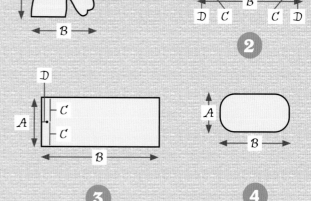

## CRAFTSMAN CHILD'S ROCKING CHAIR

### 1 ROCKER
A ⁵⁄₁₆in (8mm)
B 2¼in (57mm)

### 2 SEAT
A 1⅜in (35mm)
B 1⁵⁄₁₆in (33mm)
C 1¼in (32mm)
D ¹⁵⁄₁₆in (24mm)
E ⅛in (3mm)
F ³⁄₁₆in (4.5mm)

### 3 FRONT LEG CONSTRUCTION
A ⅜in (10mm)
B ⅜in (10mm)

### 4 BACK LEG CONSTRUCTION
A ¹⁄₁₆in (1mm)
B ⅞in (22mm)
C ³⁄₁₆in (5mm)
D ⅜in (10mm)
E ⅜in (10mm)

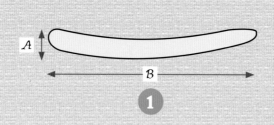

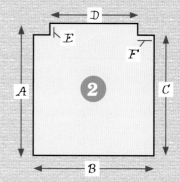

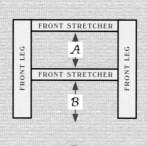

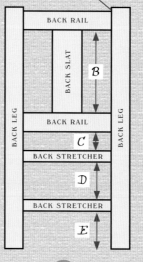

# Equipment & Materials

THIS SECTION PROVIDES INFORMATION ON THE TOOLS AND MATERIALS THAT YOU MAY BE REQUIRED TO USE TO MAKE UP THE EDWARDIAN FURNITURE AND ACCESSORIES PROJECTS. YOU MAY FIND IT USEFUL TO READ THROUGH THESE PAGES BEFORE BEGINNING TO WORK ON ANY OF THE PROJECTS.

## GLUES

**PLASTICS GLUE**
Use specifically to fix plastic components together.

**SUPER GLUE GEL**
A strong glue, non runny, which bonds instantly.

**TACKY GLUE**
A non-toxic, water-based glue that dries clear, strong and flexible. It is recommended throughout the book and is particularly suited to wood, paper, card and fabric.

## SAFETY ADVICE

ENSURE THAT SHARP TOOLS ARE HANDLED CAREFULLY AND STORED SAFELY.

ALWAYS WEAR A DUST MASK WHEN SANDING WOOD TO AVOID INHALING FINE DUST PARTICLES.

FOLLOW THE MANUFACTURER'S SAFETY INSTRUCTIONS AND ALWAYS ENSURE GOOD VENTILATION WHEN USING OIL- AND WAX-BASED PRODUCTS AND SUPER GLUE GEL.

# BASIC CRAFTING TOOLS

GENERAL CRAFTING TOOLS ARE USEFUL FOR MANY OF THE PROJECTS IN THIS BOOK.

### CRAFT KNIFE

Used for cutting wood and card. Always use with a cutting mat and steel ruler.

### CUTTING MAT

A mat must be used when cutting with a craft knife to protect working surfaces.

### EMBOSSING TOOL

A hand-held tool with ball-shaped ends that create raised designs when used with metal embossing sheets.

### PAINTBRUSHES

Use artists' paintbrushes to apply paint and varnishes. They are available in a range of sizes.

### PAPER PUNCH

Used to cut out shapes from paper and thin card. Available in craft shops in a variety of shapes and sizes.

### PLIERS

Small pliers are useful for holding tiny components.

### RULER

An essential basic tool used for accurate measuring and cutting. Always use a steel ruler when cutting with a craft knife.

### SCISSORS

Essential for cutting craft materials.

### SCORING TOOL

A tool used to make indentations into a surface. A ballpoint pen, without ink, is a perfect scoring tool.

### TUBE BENDER

A coiled wire tool used for shaping brass and aluminium tube. Available from model shops.

### WIRE CUTTERS

A tool used to cut wire safely.

*Embossing tool*

*Pliers*

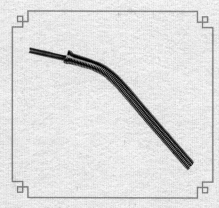

*Tube bender*

# Woodworking Tools

T HE FOLLOWING TOOLS ARE RECOMMENDED TO MAKE WORKING WITH WOOD ACCURATE AND SAFE:

## CLAMPS
Ideal for holding wooden objects in position while the glue dries.

## MITRE CUTTERS
A hand-held tool that will cut and mitre strip wood up to ½in (13mm) thick. They are generally used as an alternative to a saw and mitre block.

## NEEDLE FILES
These have fine, shaped tips for intricate shaping and sanding.

## PIN VICE
Used to hold extremely fine drill bits up to ⅛in (3mm) diameter and is used to drill through wood.

## RIGHT-ANGLED GLUING JIG
A frame, often homemade, with two fixed sides set at right-angles to ensure that the object is held square while the glue dries.

## SANDPAPER
Also known as abrasive paper and used for smoothing wood available in a range of grades. Fine-grade sandpaper is used for most projects in this book.

## SAW AND MITRE BLOCK
To cut and mitre strip wood and metal tubing. Use a razor saw or junior hacksaw together with a small metal or plastic mitre box.

## STEEL WOOL
Fine-grade steel wire wool should be used to apply beeswax to wood.

*Mitre cutters*

*Needle file*

*Right-angled gluing jig*

# WOOD

**M**ANY OF THE PROJECTS IN THIS BOOK ARE MADE FROM WOOD AND THIS SECTION LISTS THE WOOD USED. YOU MAY SUBSTITUTE ANY OF THE WOOD IF YOU WISH, BUT DO KEEP TO THE SAME WOOD TYPE DURING A PROJECT FOR BEST RESULTS.

## BASS WOOD
A white-coloured hard wood with a fine straight grain.

## MAHOGANY
A reddish brown hardwood with a straight, fine and even grain.

## OBECHI WOOD
A pale yellow-coloured wood with an open grain. It is one of the lightest hardwoods available, making it ideal for model making.

## PLYWOOD
This is made from thin sheets of wood veneer, stacked and glued so that the grain direction alternates with each layer to prevent warping and twisting.

## WOOD DOWEL
Cylindrical and available in various diameters.

## WOOD DRAWER KNOBS
Turned knobs are available in various sizes.

## WOOD MOULDING
Can be cut to produce decorative framing and edging to projects.

## WOOD SPINDLES
These are available in a variety of shapes and sizes.

Bass

Spindle

Moulding

Mahogany

Obechi

Drawer knobs

Plywood

Dowel

# PRIMING, COLOURING & FINISHING MATERIALS

THE VARIOUS PRIMING, COLOURING AND FINISHING MEDIUMS USED THROUGHOUT THE BOOK WILL HELP TO PRODUCE AN AUTHENTIC APPEARANCE TO THE EDWARDIAN PROJECTS. PLEASE REFER TO BASIC TECHNIQUES ON PAGE 179 FOR APPLICATION DETAILS.

## BEESWAX POLISH

A scented polish, which is applied to wood to create a soft sheen.

## METAL PRIMER

This is applied to metal surfaces as a base coat to prevent rusting and to help the paint to adhere.

## PAINTS

Water-based acrylic paints are recommended for the painted projects, as they are non-toxic and quick drying. Glass and enamel paints are also available in acrylics. Several of the projects require oil-based spray paints (see safety tips on page 169).

## PENCILS

HB pencils are ideal.

## SANDING SEALER

A medium applied to wood, to seal and smooth the surface.

## VARNISH

A water-based or oil-based medium that gives a shiny finish when dry. (Clear nail-varnish can be used as an alternative). Available also in satin and matt for duller finishes. 3D gloss varnish is a rubber-stamping accessory and produces a raised glossy finish.

## WOOD STAIN

Available water-based or oil-based to colour wood.

Beeswax polish

Acrylic paint

Enamel paint

Spray paint

Varnish

Wood stain

*Aluminium tube*

*Cocktail sticks*

*Brass tube*

# SPECIALIST MATERIALS

Some of the more specialized materials required to complete the Edwardian projects in this book are covered here. Suppliers are listed on page 180.

*Appliqué pins*

*Beads*

*Belaying pins*

*Centre cane*

*Brads*

## ADHESIVE TAPE
Available one-sided or double-sided from craft or office suppliers. Aluminium adhesive tape is available from car accessory shops

## ALUMINIUM EMBOSSING SHEET
A soft, malleable metal sheet used for craft work. Thin aluminium foil from foil food containers can be used as an alternative.

## ALUMINIUM TUBE
A hollow tube available in a range of diameters from model shops.

## APPLIQUE PINS
Fine, short pins available from haberdashery (notions) stores.

## BEADS
Various beads are used. Specific details and a photograph of the beads required are shown for each project.

## BELAYING PIN
A wooden, model-shipbuilding component, which is available from model shops.

## BRADS
Paper fasteners used in craft projects.

## BRASS EMBOSSING SHEET
A soft, malleable metal sheet used for craft work.

## BRASS TUBE AND ROD
Available in a range of diameters from model shops.

## CARD
Available from art and craft shops in a variety of colours and thicknesses.

## CENTRE CANE
Used in basket-making and available in various thicknesses.

Cord

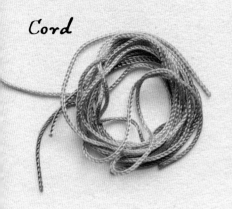

Cotter pins

Double columns

Eyelets

Grain-of-wheat bulb

Hardware

## COCKTAIL STICKS

Often used as a substitute for $\frac{3}{32}$in (2.5mm) hardwood dowel. Cocktail sticks with turned ends are called 'fancy-ended' cocktail sticks.

## CORD

Made from twisted threads and available in a range of thicknesses from haberdashery (notions) stores.

## COTTER PIN

A split metal fastening pin available from teddy bear making suppliers.

## DOUBLE COLUMN

A wooden, model-shipbuilding component, available from model shops.

## ETCHED BRASS METAL LEAVES

Available from specialists in miniatures.

## EYELETS

Use straight-ended metal eyelets. These are measured by the narrow opening at one end and available from craft shops.

## FABRIC

For best results, always use fine cotton fabric.

## FELT

Thin adhesive felt is recommended and is available from craft suppliers.

## FILIGREES AND FINDINGS

Metal egg-decorating components, including shades, caps and bells.

## FLORAL TAPE

Used in cake decorating to bind leaf and flower stems together.

## GRAIN-OF-WHEAT BULBS

Available from miniature lighting specialists.

## HAMA BEADS

Colourful plastic beads generally used by children.

## HARDWARE

Handles, knobs and pins are available from miniature hardware specialists.

## JEWELLERY FINDINGS

Metal components for jewellery making, including bead caps and jump rings.

Hama beads

Floral tape

Filigrees, findings and jewellery findings

Leather

Polymer clay

Twine

**LEATHER**
Thin glove leather is the most manageable to use for working in miniature.

**MASKING TAPE**
A strong tape, adhesive on one side, available from hardware stores.

**MIRROR**
Small glass mirrors are available in a range of shapes and sizes from craft shops. Alternatively, thin plastic sheet-mirror can be cut to size using scissors.

**PAPER**
Available from art and craft shops in a range of colours, thicknesses and textures.

**PEWTER EMBOSSING SHEET**
A soft, malleable metal sheet used for craft work.

**POLYMER CLAY**
A modelling clay that can be baked in domestic ovens to make items solid and long lasting.

**POM POMS**
Tiny, fluffy balls available from haberdashery (notions) stores.

**RIVET CONTACTS**
Available from miniature lighting specialists. Usually used to promote good electrical conductivity.

**SEQUIN PINS**
Generally used in the projects for hinging. Available from haberdashery (notions) stores

**STYRENE TUBE AND ROD**
Available in a range of diameters from model shops.

**THREADS**
Various threads are used in the projects. Available from haberdashery (notions) stores.

**TWINE**
Available from garden centres, either natural or coloured.

**WADDING**
Used to provide padding to cushions. Available in various thicknesses from haberdashery (notions) stores.

**WIRE**
Jewellery-making plated wire and paper-covered wire (normally used in cake decoration) are available in various gauges and colours.

Sequin pins

Pom poms

Rivet contacts

Styrene tube

Thread

Wire

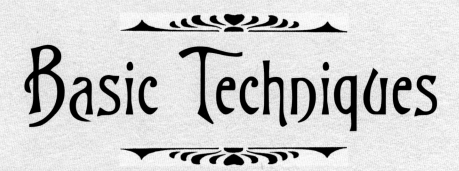

# Basic Techniques

This section will help you become familiar with the basic techniques frequently used throughout the book and it is advisable to read through this before starting on the projects. Please also refer to the important safety advice (page **169**).

## TRANSFERRING TEMPLATES

Many of the projects have templates, which can be found on pages **153** to **168**. Follow these procedures to accurately transfer measurements and images from the templates pages.

### TRANSFERRING MEASUREMENTS
Transfer measurements from templates using a ruler and pencil. Never mix imperial and metric measurements – always use one or the other.

### TRANSFERRING IMAGES
All other images can be photocopied, or scanned into a computer and printed for accuracy, or traced with a pencil and tracing paper.

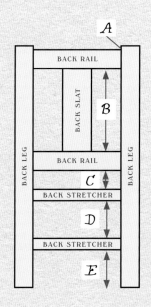

# WORKING WITH WOOD

**M**ANY OF THE PROJECTS IN THIS BOOK HAVE WOOD AS THEIR MAIN COMPONENT. FOLLOWING THESE PROCEDURES SHOULD ENSURE THAT YOUR WOOD PIECES WILL FIT TOGETHER PERFECTLY.

## CUTTING WOOD

Wood can be cut using a craft knife and metal ruler, a saw and mitre block, or mitre cutters. Always cut the wood with the grain running in line with the sides that have the longest measurement, unless instructed otherwise.

## SANDING WOOD

Always use fine-grade sandpaper, unless instructed otherwise, to remove any burr from the ends of wood and to smooth. Take care not to oversand and alter the shape and size of the wood as wood pieces will not fit together correctly.

## CHAMFERING

This term means creating a sloping edge to a piece of wood. Create this effect by holding a piece of wood at a slight angle, with the edge to be chamfered positioned above fine-grade sandpaper. Sand the edge in small sweeping motions in the same direction, until the correct angle is achieved. Most projects do not require specific angles to be chamfered and this technique is generally used for appearance only.

## MORTISE AND TENON JOINTS

A mortise and tenon joint was commonly used in American Craftsman-style furniture and is basically a hole (mortise) in one piece of wood into which a shaped second piece of wood (tenon) fits to form a mortise and tenon joint.

## REBATE

A recess cut in a length of wood for framing is known as a rebate.

## MITRING AND FRAMING

The term 'mitre' is used to describe the right-angled joint made between two pieces of wood, when the ends have been cut to an angle of 45 degrees and fitted together. This can be achieved using either a mitre block and razor saw, positioning the saw in the diagonal openings of the mitre block to cut through the wood at an angle, or using mitre cutters and pressing the wood against the guide to achieve a 45-degree angle cut (see also page 171).

To make a frame, mitre the ends of two matching pairs of picture frame moulding, ensuring that the recess on the wood pieces run in line with the shortest length of the mitred wood strip. Position the corresponding size lengths opposite each other in a right-angled gluing jig (page 171) and glue together.

*Chamfering*

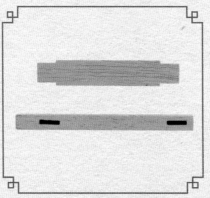

*Mortise and tenon joint*

*Mitred joint*

# USING COLOURING AND FINISHING MEDIUMS

IN ORDER TO RE-CREATE AN AUTHENTIC EDWARDIAN STYLE TO YOUR PROJECTS YOU WILL NEED TO TREAT THE SURFACES OF THE MODELS TO VARIOUS COLOURING AND FINISHING MEDIUMS. DIRECTIONS AND TECHNIQUES FOR APPLYING THE MEDIUMS ARE DETAILED HERE.

## BEESWAX POLISH

Apply beeswax polish to finished articles, unless otherwise advised, using fine-gauge wire wool and then buff to a sheen using a clean soft cloth. Use a small stiff paintbrush to apply the beeswax polish to awkward areas.

## PAINTS

Apply two thin coats of paint with a paintbrush, allowing the first coat to dry in between, to avoid the components warping. When using acrylic paints, achieve a smooth painted surface by very lightly sanding the surfaces on all sides to smooth the finish of the paint. If necessary, re-paint and repeat the procedure. Buff the pieces to produce a dull sheen using a piece of kitchen paper towel. Several of the projects use oil-based spray or enamel paints; follow the manufacturer's safety advice when using these products.

## VARNISH

Apply two thin coats of varnish using a paintbrush, allowing the first coat to dry in between. 3D gloss varnish should be applied in a thicker layer and all air bubbles should be removed before leaving to dry.

## WOOD STAIN

Use a soft cloth to apply wood stain sparingly, as too much stain can warp the wood. Always stain the components before assembly and allow them to dry completely.

# DISTRESSING TECHNIQUES

CERTAIN TECHNIQUES CAN BE USED TO IMITATE AGE OR WEAR AND TEAR TO A SURFACE. STAINED WOOD IN PARTICULAR RESPONDS WELL TO DISTRESSING TREATMENTS.

## DRY BRUSHING

One of the ways this technique is used in the book is to create the effect of water damage on wooden surfaces. Apply a small amount of acrylic paint on to a dry, medium-sized paintbrush and then remove the paint on a dry rag. Use the paintbrush to brush over the article to give a 'whisper' or subtle dusting of the paint. Build up layers of white and pale grey colours using the dry brushing technique to produce effective results. Use the same process with shades of grey paint for a sooty effect on the fireplaces.

Dry brushing

# Suppliers

## UK

### BEAD EXCLUSIVE
Nixon House
119-121 Teignmouth Road
Torquay
South Devon
TQ1 4HA
Tel: +44 (0)1803 322 000
**www.bead-exclusive.co.uk**
Beads, jewellery findings and wire

### FRED ALDOUS
37 Lever Street
Manchester
M1 1LW
Tel: +44 (0)161 236 4224
**www.fredaldous.co.uk**
General craft supplies, tools, haberdashery and art
materials

### GEORGINA RITSON
Email: info@dollsbygeorginaritson.co.uk
Tel: +44 (0)207 482 2488
**www.dollsbygeorginaritson.co.uk**
Dolls

### IRONWORKS
240 Doxey
Stafford
Staffordshire
ST16 1EE
Tel: +44 (0)1785 243 494
**www.ironworks-miniatures.co.uk**
Miniature hardware

### JANE HARROP
4 Buckingham Road
Poynton
Cheshire
SK12 1JH
**www.janeharrop.co.uk**
Tel: +44 (0)1625 873 117
Edwardian furniture kits, belaying pins, double columns,
washer beads, 3mm eyelets, tacky glue

### JENNIFER'S OF WALSALL
5 Appledore Terrace (Off Daffodil Road)
Orchard Hills
Walsall
West Midlands
WS5 3DU
Tel: +44 (0)1922 616 298
**www.jennifersofwalsall.co.uk**
Wood, miniature lighting components, tools, plastic mirror,
hardware and tools, wallpaper

### LITTLE TRIMMINGS
PO Box 2267
Reading
RG4 8WG
Tel: +44 (0)8452 269 751
**www.littletrimmings.com**
Small-scale haberdashery and fabrics

## TEE PEE CRAFTS
White Cottage
40 High Street
Eagle
Lincolnshire
LN6 9DG
Tel: +44 (0)1522 868 270
**www.teepeecrafts.co.uk**
Egg decorating findings and filigrees, beads, brass tube,
plastic mirror

## THE BEAD CELLAR
Broad Street,
Black Torrington
Devon
EX21 5PT
Tel: +44 (0)1409 231 442
**www.thebeadcellar.co.uk**
Beads, jewellery findings, threads and wires

## WOOD SUPPLIES
Monkey Puzzle Cottage
53 Woodmansterne Lane
Wallington
Surrey
SM6 0SW
Tel: +44 (0)20 8669 7266 (eves)
Wood and wood mouldings

# USA

## DICK BLICK ART MATERIALS
P.O. Box 1267
Galesburg
IL 61402-1267
Tel: +1 (800) 828 4548
**www.dickblick.com**
Tools, paper punches, paper, card, adhesives and jewellery
findings

## DOLLHOUSE COLLECTABLES
29 Wren Street
Litchfield
NH 03052
Tel: +1 (800) 799 9680
**www.dollhousecollectables.com**
Wood, miniature lighting components, hardware and tools

## FIRE MOUNTAIN GEMS AND BEADS
One Fire Mountain Way
Grants Pass
OR 97526-2373
Tel: +1 (800) 355 2137
**www.firemountaingems.com**
Beads, jewellery findings, threads and wires

## NATURE COAST HOBBIES, INC.
6773 S. Hancock Road
Homosassa
FL 34448
Tel: +1 (352) 628 3990
**www.naturecoast.com**
Belaying pins, double columns and tools

# BIBLIOGRAPHY

Arber, Katie
**Turn of the Century Style**
Middlesex University Press, 2003
ISBN 978 1 89825 387 0

Bell, Yvonne
**The Edwardian Home**
Shire Publications Limited, 2005
ISBN 978 0 74780 631 4

Bishop, Christina
**Miller's Collecting Kitchenware**
Octopus Publishing Group Limited,
1995
ISBN 978 1 84000 254 9

Hardy, William & Adams, Steven &
Van de Lemme, Arie
**The Encyclopedia of Decorative
Styles 1850–1935**
Quintet Publishing Limited, 1999
ISBN 978 0 86288 287 7

Hockman, Hilary
**Edwardian House Style Handbook**
David & Charles, 2001
ISBN 978 0 71531 227 8

Long, Helen
**The Edwardian House**
Manchester University Press, 1993
ISBN 978 0 71903 729 8

Mack, Lorrie
**The Home Styling Source Book**
Carlton Books Limited, 2001
ISBN 978 1 84222 299 6

McCrum, Mark & Sturgis, Matthew
**1900 House**
Channel 4 Books, 2000
ISBN 978 0 75227 228 4

Miller, Judith
**Decorative Arts: Style & Design
From Classical to Contemporary**
Dorling Kindersley Limited, 2006
ISBN 978 1 40531 290 4

Miller, Judith & Martin
**Period Style**
Mitchell Beazley, 1993
ISBN 978 1 85732 301 7

Osband, Linda
**Victorian House Style**
David & Charles, 1997
ISBN 978 0 71539 841 5

Yorke, Trevor
**The Edwardian House Explained**
Countryside Books, 2006
ISBN 978 1 85306 982 5

**Decorative Tile Designs**
Dover Publications, Inc. 2005
ISBN 978 0 48699 648 4

**Making Authentic Craftsman
Furniture: Instructions and Plans
for 62 Projects**
Articles from 'The Craftsman', edited by
Gustav Stickley and published between
1901 and 1916
Dover publications, Inc. 1986
ISBN 978 0 48625 000 8

**Times past magazine collection**
Marshall Cavendish Limited, 1987/8

## ABOUT THE AUTHOR

Jane Harrop has been making miniatures for seventeen years. She has previously written two miniatures books for the publishers David and Charles, and **Thirties & Forties Miniatures in 1/12th scale** for the Guild of Master Craftsman publishers. She displays and sells her work through her website (www.janeharrop.co.uk) and through miniatures fairs. She stocks a good range of wooden furniture kits for many of the projects in her books for those who don't like cutting wood, but still enjoy being creative. She shares her knowledge and enthusiasm on the subject by teaching regular adult education classes and also presents workshops around the country and online. Jane is married with two daughters, and lives in Cheshire, UK.

## ACKNOWLEDGEMENTS

I firstly must thank Bob Williams for his constant support and advice, especially when some of the projects' measurements got a bit tricky and also John Wallace for advice on technical terms. Thank you also to all of my adult education class learners who spent two very busy terms constructing, decorating and furnishing an Edwardian dolls house with many of the projects in this book. I appreciated your dedication and continued enthusiasm as we progressed through the stages of the course, you all worked so hard. Thank you to Georgina Ritson for her lovely dolls (details on page 180) and also to all the makers of the accessories used to complement the Edwardian pieces in this book. Finally, thank you to everyone at Guild of Master Craftsman Publications.

L

leather 176

Letter opener **67, 69**

living rooms 52

M

Magnifying glass **67, 69**

mahogany 172

masking tape 176

materials

specialist 174–6

wood 172

measurements 9, 177

metal primer 173

mirrors 176

mitre cutters 171

mitring 178

Morris, William 54, 58

mortise and tenon joints 178

N

needle files 171

O

obechi wood 172

Over-mantel mirror **46–7**

P

paintbrushes 170

paints 173, 179

Palette knife **105, 107**

paper 176

paper punches 170

Paperclip **67, 68**

Pastry board **105, 107**

Pastry brush **105, 106**

Pedestal cake stand **40, 41**

Pen **66, 68**

Pen wipe **66, 67**

Pencil **66, 68**

pewter embossing sheets 176

pin vices 171

Plant stand **18–19**

template 153

plastics glue 169

Plate rack **92–3**

pliers 170

plywood 172

polymer clay 176

pom poms 176

Pot pourri dish **117, 118**

Potted fern plant **20–1**

leaf template 153

priming mediums 173

Pull horse **148–9**

templates 168

R

rebates 178

Reception room fireplace **42–5**

templates 157–8

right-angled gluing jigs 171

rivet contacts 176

Rocker blotter **66, 68**

Rolling pin **105, 106**

rulers 170

S

safety 169

sanding sealer 173

sanding wood 169, 178

sandpaper 171

saucepans 104

saw and mitre block 171

scale 9

scissors 170

scoring tools 170

Seal and sealing wax **67, 69**

Sears, Roebuck and Company 36

sequin pins 176

Silver-lidded scent bottles **117, 119**

Sink and draining board **89–91**

templates 161

steel wool 171

Stickley, Gustav 25

styrene tubes and rods 176

super glue gel 169

T

Tabletop mirror **139–41**

template 167

tacky glue 169

templates 153–68

transferring 177

threads 176

Tiffany, Louis Comfort 78

Tiffany table lamp **78–9**

Tiny cut glass scent bottles **118, 119**

tools

crafting 170

woodworking 171

transferring templates 177

Trivet **40, 41**

tube benders 170

twine 176

V

varnish 173, 179

Vase of roses **48–9**

W

wadding 176

Wall shelves **76–7**

template 160

Wardrobe **127–31**

templates 166

Washstand **132, 142–3**

templates 167

Whisk **105, 106**

wire 176

wire cutters 170

wood 172, 178

wood dowel 172

wood drawer knobs 172

wood moulding 172

wood spindles 172

wood stain 173, 179

woodworking tools 171

TO PLACE AN ORDER, OR TO
REQUEST A CATALOGUE,
PLEASE CONTACT:

GMC Publications
Castle Place, 166 High Street,
Lewes, East Sussex,
BN7 1XU, United Kingdom
• Tel: +44 (0)1273 488005 •
• Fax: +44 (0)1273 402866 •
www.gmcbooks.com

# Index

Projects are shown in **Bold**

## A

adhesive tape 174
adhesives see glues
aluminium embossing sheet 174
aluminiun tube 174
American Arts & Crafts
    movement 34
appliqué pins 174
Art Nouveau 9, 12, 32, 52
Arts & Crafts corner sofa **54–7**
    templates 159
Arts & Crafts desk chair **64–5**
    templates 160
Arts & Crafts gramophone table
    **74–5**
    template 160
Arts & Craft hallstand **14–17**
    templates 153
Arts & Craft lady's writing desk
    **50, 61–3**
    templates 160
Arts & Crafts movement
    9, 12, 32, 52
Arts & Crafts occasional table
    **28–9**
    templates 155
Arts & Crafts reclining
    armchair **50, 58–60**
attic rooms 134

## B

bass wood 172
beads 174
Bedroom fireplace **123–6**
    templates 165
bedrooms 110
beeswax polish 173, 179

belaying pins 174
Bell **66, 67**
Bonbon stand **40, 41**
Bottles with glass stoppers
    **117, 118**
Bowls and stands **40–1**
brads 174
brass embossing sheet 174
brass tubes and rods 174
Brownie box camera **80–1**
Button hook **118, 119**

## C

Capstan inkwell **66, 67**
Cast-iron single bed **144–7**
centre cane 174
chamfering 178
Chest of drawers **132, 136–8**
    templates 167
clamps 171
cocktail sticks 175
colouring 173, 179
cord 175
cotter pins 175
craft knives 170
crafting tools 170
Craftsman child's rocking
    chair **150–2**
    templates 168
Craftsman dining chair
    **30, 36–7**
    templates 156
Craftsman dining table
    **30, 34–5**
    templates 156
Craftsman hall bench **10, 25–7**
    templates 154

Craftsman serving table **38–9**
    template 156
Cut glass storage jars **117, 118**
cutting mats 170
cutting wood 178

## D

Decorative metalware **10, 22–4**
    templates 153
Desk accessories **66–9**
dining rooms 32
distressing techniques 179
Double bed **108, 120–2**
double column 175
Dressing table **108, 112–16**
    templates 164
Dressing table accessories
    **117–19**
dry brushing 179

## E

Eastman Kodak Company 80
Edison, Thomas 70
Edwardian era 8
embossing tools 170
etched brass metal leaves 175
eyelets 175

## F

fabric 175
felt 175
filigrees and findings 175
finishing 173, 179
floral tape 175
framing 178
Fruit bowl **40, 41**

## G

glues 169
grain-of-wheat bulbs 175

Gramophone **70–3**
    templates 160
Grater **105, 107**
    templates 163

## H

hallways 12
hama beads 175
hardware 175
Hat pins **118, 119**
Hat-pin holder **118, 119**

## I

imperial and metric
    measurements 9, 177

## J

jewellery findings 175

## K

Kitchen dresser **82, 94–7**
    templates 162
Kitchen fireplace surround
    **98–9**
    templates 162
Kitchen range **100–4**
    templates 163
Kitchen table **82, 86–8**
    templates 161
kitchens 84
Kitchenware **105–7**
    templates 163